Twayne's United States Authors Series

Sylvia E. Bowman, *Editor*

INDIANA UNIVERSITY

Dion Boucicault

Dion Boucicault

By ROBERT HOGAN

University of California, Davis

 163

Twayne Publishers, Inc.   ::   New York

Preface

"Dion Boucicault!"

That was how Townsend Walsh began his 1914 biography of the famous nineteenth-century dramatist. Today, more than seventy-five years after Boucicault's death, we should probably have to replace Walsh's exclamation mark with a question mark. The great resurgence of dramatic activity that began in the last quarter of the last century with Ibsen, and that shows no sign as yet of abating, has made the theater of Boucicault seem to the modern temper almost absurdly naïve. Douglas Jerrold, Bulwer-Lytton, Tom Taylor, H. J. Byron, Augustin Daly, Sydney Grundy, and even Tom Robertson are already half-forgotten names from an insignificant period. But even now the name of Boucicault can conjure up for a few theatrical buffs a memory of delight, of excitement, and of magic.

And they would be right, for Boucicault was a theatrical magician of the first order. A magician, I take it, is a man who evokes wonder and delight from his audience; and this is exactly what Boucicault did for half a century. But, unless we really believe in magic, we think of the magician as evoking wonder and delight by sleight-of-hand. We know that the woman in the cabinet has not really been wafted off into the fourth dimension; we know that the man is not really sawed in half and miraculously rejoined. It is just that, for one startled minute, they seem to have been.

A dramatist, like a magician, is a clever trickster and sometimes even something of a charlatan. The great dramatists—the Sophocles, the Shakespeare, the Shaw—by the magnificence of their rhetoric, the music of their words, the quality of their fancy, or the wonder of their wit manage to trick us into a real, although probably momentary, perception of the essence of things. And the quality of that trick is so superb that we rank the works of a

Sophocles, a Shakespeare, and a Shaw among the great accomplishments of man.

The tricks of a popular minor dramatist like Boucicault are simpler, more obvious, less original and individual—perhaps even a bit tawdry, a bit shopworn. But any dramatist, whether a Shakespeare or a Boucicault, tricks his audience into accepting a simplified sketch of life for its complex reality. That probably is where a consideration of Boucicault, or practically any other dramatist, must begin.

The drama's medium is, at least partly, words; and so drama has some claim to be treated as literature. However, the words are spoken, and the emotions they suggest are mimed. The drama's real place is on the stage rather than on the page, and the stage has a set of standards quite its own. Those theatrical standards are always somewhat different and sometimes completely different from the standards of pure literature. Most dramatic criticism, however, treats plays solely as works of literature, and is frequently a very inappropriate commentary. What we usually consider the great plays—say, Sophocles' *Oedipus Rex*, Shakespeare's *Hamlet*, Bernard Shaw's *Saint Joan*—exist as both literature and theater. For that matter, so do a handful of Boucicault's plays. But the great mass of plays, even good ones, have little standing as literature. The excellence of Brandon Thomas' famous old farce *Charley's Aunt* or Mrs. Henry Wood's popular old melodrama *East Lynne* is purely theatrical. Their only memorable lines are, respectively, "I'm from Brazil where the nuts come from" and "Dead! And he never called me mother!" As literary examples of comic and tragic discourse, these lines are, to put it mildly, inadequate; but, as theatrical speech, they are faultless.

In other words, we cannot dissect *Charley's Aunt* by the standards appropriate for William Congreve's masterpiece *The Way of the World*. The one has no standing as literature, and the other has never been very successful theater. Boucicault's plays must also be judged primarily as theater, and the majority of them must even be judged as pieces of theatrical entertainment rather than of theatrical art.

To critical minds honed on Fyodor Dostoevsky, Henry James, or James Joyce, theatrical criticism can only seem an intellectual debasement. No doubt such a view is correct, and the stage is really one of the more naïve forms of art. Ibsen, Shaw, Elmer

Rice, and Denis Johnston have been among the very few modern dramatists who have attempted to lessen that naïveté, and their attempt is one firm reason for their excellence. However, many other fine modern dramatists, like J. M. Synge and Sean O'Casey and Eugene O'Neill, have never used a play for an intellectually complex statement. Synge wrote, "The drama is made serious . . . not by the degree in which it is taken up with problems that are serious in themselves, but by the degree in which it gives the nourishment . . . on which our imaginations live." And again, "The drama, like the symphony, does not teach or prove anything." [1]

I personally prefer a drama like Shaw's *Back to Methuselah* to one like Boucicault's *The Colleen Bawn;* and Denis Johnston's *The Scythe and the Sunset* seems to me in some ways preferable to O'Casey's masterly *The Plough and the Stars.* But Shaw and, to a lesser extent, Johnston are asking for an audience of He-Ancients and She-Ancients, when most audiences are still only emotional children. And that fact is the way of the world of the stage.

Probably we should remember, then, when considering Boucicault, that this simple emotionalism of the conventional stage is not to be despised. There are at least two kinds of knowledge —that which comes from intellectual perception and that from emotional perception. The signs of emotional perception are, among others, an intolerable sense of anguish or a pervasive and ebullient joy. Such emotional reactions were aroused by the simple statements of a Boucicault play. Perhaps today a good deal of Boucicault would be rejected as too naïve; if so, that would seem a healthy sign for the human race. Some of Boucicault, I am convinced, is still valid in the theater, and probably it shall continue to be valid until humans are hatched from Shavian eggs. Until that day when Boucicault—and, for that matter, Sophocles, Shakespeare, O'Casey, and O'Neill—shall be swept into the intellectual dustbin as the toys of our nonage, he retains a certain artistic value in the theater and a certain human importance outside it.

I have not in this study given critical attention to every known play by Boucicault. If I had, the book would be several times as long, and have even less claim to value than it now does. I have given most attention to those plays which, by common consent, are his best. I have, however, discussed a typical selection of his potboiling successes, in order to illustrate what most Boucicault plays are like.

I am considerably indebted in this study to the previous researches of Townsend Walsh, Julius H. Tolson, and Boucicault's great-grandson Christopher Calthrop. I have also profited by the critical remarks of Micheál Ó h Aodha and David Krause, and by the brilliant Abbey Theatre production of *The Shaughraun*. James Kormier, one of my students at the University of California, gave me much aid in compiling the Bibliography. Mainly, however, it was Sean O'Casey's contagious enthusiasm for Boucicault that turned me to this study, and I hope that some tincture of that great man's spirit may linger over its pages.

Robert Hogan

University of California, Davis

Contents

Chronology

1820   December 7, December 26, December 27, all possible dates for the birth of Dionysius Lardner Boursiquot, in Dublin; nominally the last child of Samuel Smith Boursiquot, wine merchant, and Anne Maria Darley; possibly the illegitimate son of Dr. Dionysius Lardner, encyclopedist.

1822   December 20, December 26, also possible dates of Boucicault's birth.

ca. 1829–1833   Probably attending school in Hampstead kept by Mr. Hessey.

1833–1835   Attending University College School, University of London.

1837   Attending a "Collegiate School" in Brentford kept by Dr. Jamieson; directs and acts in school performance of *Pizarro;* writes first play, *Napoleon's Old Guard;* probably returns to London and is apprenticed to Dr. Lardner.

1838   Runs away to Cheltenham, probably in the spring, and is employed by Charles Hill in his acting company; from July 30 to the end of the year plays in Brighton under the stage name of "Lee Moreton," acting mainly Irish roles; October 1, his first produced play, *A Legend of the Devil's Dyke*, performed at Brighton Theatre.

1839   March 9, London acting debut as "Lee Moreton" in his unpublished farcical interlude *Lodgings to Let* at the Haymarket; various provincial engagements.

1840   March 13, Lardner elopes with Mary, wife of Captain Richard Heaviside. In November, Boucicault's farce *A Lover by Proxy* rejected by Charles Mathews, but Boucicault is encouraged to write a modern comedy. In December, *London Assurance* is accepted by Mathews.

1841   March 4, *London Assurance* by "Lee Moreton" produced at Covent Garden and played sixty-nine nights.

1842– Boucicault living in London, and has seventeen or eight-
1844   een plays produced under his own name.

1845   July 9, Boucicault marries Anne Guiot in London; probably late in August he and his wife leave for the Continent.

1846   Four or five plays produced in London.

1847   In June, applied to Court of Bankruptcy, London; petition dismissed; possibly returns to France where he may have used the name of Viscount de Bourcicault.

1848   Anne, his wife, probably dies sometime this year; November 8, Boucicault appears in Insolvent Debtors Court.

1850   October 16, Agnes Robertson makes her London debut at the Princess under Charles Kean's management; Boucicault engaged by Kean as literary adviser.

1852   June 14, Boucicault plays, under his own name, the lead in his potboiler *The Vampire* at the Princess; sometime before this production, Boucicault had married Agnes Robertson, or at least begun living with her.

1853   Early August, Agnes sails for New York; September 18, Boucicault arrives in New York; October 22, Agnes' successful New York debut at Burton's.

1854   Agnes appears in various Boucicault plays in New York, Boston, Chicago, Philadelphia, Washington, D. C., Buffalo, and elsewhere; September 22, Boucicault's first appearance on the American stage, in Boston, as "Sir Patrick O' Plenipo" in *The Irish Artist;* November 10, Boucicault's New York debut as "Sir Charles Coldstream" in *Used Up.*

1855   May 10, the Boucicaults' first child, Dion William, born in New Orleans.

1856   August 18, Congress passes a copyright law as a result of cumulative efforts by Robert Montgomery Bird, George Henry Boker, and Boucicault.

1857   October 10, second child, Eve, born in New York; December 8, *The Poor of New York* produced at Wallack's, New York.

1859   May 23, third child, Darley George (Dot), born in

New York; December 6, *The Octoroon* produced at the Winter Garden, New York.

1860   March 29, *The Colleen Bawn* produced at Keene's, New York; July 17, the Boucicaults sail for England; September 10, the Boucicaults open at the Adelphi, London, in *The Colleen Bawn* which runs for 278 performances, at that time a record.

1861   April 1, the Boucicaults open in *The Colleen Bawn* at the Theatre Royal, Hawkins Street, Dublin.

1862   From June 23, Boucicault the lessee of Drury Lane; August 9, fourth child, Patrice, born in London; December 22, Astley's Amphitheatre in Westminster Bridge Road, remodeled and rechristened the Theatre Royal, is opened by Boucicault.

1863   June 12, collapse of the Theatre Royal enterprise; Boucicault, bankrupt again, leaves for Liverpool to stage *The Poor of Liverpool*.

1864   November 7, *Arrah-na-Pogue* produced at the Old Theatre Royal, Hawkins Street, Dublin.

1865   March 22, revised *Arrah-na-Pogue* presented at the Princess, London, and runs for 164 performances; September 4, Joseph Jefferson opens at the Adelphi, London, in Boucicault's revision of *Rip Van Winkle*, which runs for 170 nights.

1866   October 6, *Flying Scud* produced at the Holborn, London, and runs for 207 nights; November 5, Henry Irving's London debut in Boucicault's *Hunted Down*.

1867   February 27, Nina (Mabel Tessie), the Boucicaults' fifth child, born in London.

1869   June 23, Aubrey Robertson, the Boucicaults' sixth child, born.

1872   In partnership with the Earl of Londesborough, Boucicault leases Covent Garden; August 29, Boucicault opens Covent Garden with *Babil and Bijou*, a fantastic spectacle by him and J. R. Planche, which loses money, but runs until March 3, 1873; September 7, Boucicault and Agnes sail for New York.

1873   The Boucicault Company, without Agnes, who has returned to London, plays in New York and on tour.

1874   November 14, *The Shaughraun,* produced at Wallack's,

New York, plays until March 27; grosses $220,076.50.

1875 September 4, Boucicault and Agnes open in *The Shaughraun* in London.

1875 January 21, Dion William, the Boucicaults' eldest son, killed in railway collision at Huntington, England; December 21, Boucicault demonstrates at Wallack's, New York, how chemicals can reduce the hazard of theater fires.

1879 Boucicault plays both in London and New York; February 10, Agnes' brief return to the New York stage in *The Colleen Bawn*, at Booth's.

1880– Boucicault plays both in England and America; Agnes'
1883 last American appearance on May 27, 1883, at the Star, New York, in *The Colleen Bawn*.

1885 May 18, the Boucicault Company presents *The Jilt* at the California Theatre, San Francisco; the Company sails for Australia where Boucicault marries Louise Thorndyke, a member of the troupe, at Sydney.

1886 July 29, *The Jilt* opens for a run of two hundred nights at the Prince of Wales, London.

1888 April 30, the Boucicault Company disbanded in Chicago, Boucicault being out of funds; Agnes granted a divorce in the summer in England; Boucicault becomes director of School of Acting for A. M. Palmer's stock company at the Madison Square Theatre, New York.

1889 January 15, formal announcement of Agnes' divorce.

1890 September, Boucicault, working on an adaptation of *The Luck of Roaring Camp*, suffers a heart attack, which is complicated by pneumonia; September 18, Boucicault dies in New York; December 19, his body transferred to Mount Hope Cemetery.

CHAPTER *1*

His Life and Times

DIONYSIUS LARDNER BOUCICAULT lived a long and very active life, much of it in the public eye as a famous playwright, actor, and manager who was not the least averse to courting publicity. So, although his wanderings took him from Dublin to London to Paris, to Switzerland and Italy, up and down the length and breadth of England and the United States, and even as far afield as Australia, there are many years of Boucicault's life in which a biographer may exactly pinpoint what he was doing on any particular day. With such a wealth of information about Boucicault in newspaper files and theatrical memoirs, it is, then, all the more surprising how shrouded in obscurity are certain periods of his life and how enigmatic a personality he remains.

I *His Birth and Paternity*

The family name of Boursiquot seems to have been of French Huguenot origin, but by the time of Dion's birth the family had probably lived in Ireland for several generations. Dion's nominal great-grandfather may have been a Peter Boursiquot who married a Mary Smith in 1739. Peter's son Samuel married a Mercy Ann Smith in 1767. Samuel's son, the dramatist's nominal father, was Samuel Smith Boursiquot who married Anne Maria Darley in 1813 or 1815.[1] The Darleys were a well-known Irish family from the Scalp in County Wicklow. One of Anne's brothers was a prominent poet George Darley who wrote several closet dramas. Another brother, the Reverend Charles Frederick Darley, had his play *Plighted Troth; or, A Woman Her Own Rival* produced at Drury Lane by Macready in 1842.[2]

The two most stubborn biographical problems are those of determining who Boucicault's father was and when Boucicault

was born. Throughout his life, Boucicault was dogged by the
rumor of illegitimacy. Julius H. Tolson thinks that there is nothing to support this theory, but Townsend Walsh makes a convincing case for Dion's having been sired by Dr. Dionysius
Lardner, a well-known professor, writer, lecturer, popularizer of
science, and encyclopedist.

Lardner was a quite interesting man, and some aspects of his
character and career are reminiscent of his namesake, the playwright. Lardner, who was born in Dublin on April 3, 1793,
took several degrees from Trinity College, Dublin, among them
an Ll.B. and an Ll.D. In July, 1827, he was appointed as the
first professor of natural philosophy and astronomy at the recently formed University of London. H. Hale Bellot in his history
of the school remarked of Lardner:

> He made up in contemporary notoriety what he lacks in more
> lasting fame. Lardner, his apparatus, his courses, and his salary,
> caused more pother than almost any other topic in the early his-
> tory of the college, and he occupied a very disproportionate amount
> of the early Minutes of the Sessions of the Council. He figured
> equally prominently in the public eye. He was a very successful
> popular lecturer, and a man of unbounded energy and great liter-
> ary activity . . . and he moved more freely than any other of the
> professors in the fashionable literary society of his time. His in-
> augural address was a sensational success. His public lectures were
> well attended and highly appreciated. And his apparatus won
> favour where the more austere learning of some of his colleagues
> failed. It gave notoriety to his lectures and afforded a diversion to
> the aristocracy. . . . His regular courses were not very successful,
> and he was discontented with the salary which he derived from
> them, and found that he could make a much larger income by lit-
> erary work. He resigned his chair in the university in 1831.[3]

Lardner wrote some mathematical and scientific treatises, but he
was best known for his hundred-and-thirty-four volume reference
work *The Cabinet Clyclopedia.* His very successful career was
interrupted, however, when he eloped to Paris in 1840 with Mrs.
Mary Heaviside, whose husband sued Lardner and received a
judgment of £8,000. Lardner's career in England never survived
the public scandal, but he is said to have recouped by a successful lecture tour in America. Much of his later life was spent on
the Continent, and he died in Naples on April 29, 1859.

There was some physical resemblance between Lardner and Boucicault, although it was not so striking, I think, as David Krause has suggested. Both were men of talent, ambition, and prolific productivity, but there was also an air of vague spuriousness that clung to the work of both of them. Dickens called Lardner "that prince of humbugs," and, of course, Boucicault garnered many similar accolades. Both were attractive and congenial companions, and both were decidedly gay dogs. Boucicault was married at least two and probably three times; Lardner, before his elopement with Mrs. Heaviside, had been married in Dublin to Cecilia Flood, had fathered three children, and had been deserted by his wife whom he eventually divorced. Boucicault, like Lardner, became embroiled in a notorious marital scandal which clouded the end of his own career. It would be stretching the point a good deal to say that such resemblances are more than mildly suggestive, but they should doubtless be mentioned.

Much less is known of Samuel Smith Boursiquot, Dion's nominal father. Like Bernard Shaw's father, Boursiquot was a Dublin merchant who failed in business and in marriage. His marriage to Anne Darley produced three earlier sons—William, Arthur, and George—and apparently a daughter who died in 1831. Townsend Walsh, after describing Samuel and the previous Boursiquots as "mediocrities," goes on to say:

> Mr. Arthur Darley, a well-known Irish musician of the present day [ca. 1915], living at Rathgar, Dublin, and a collateral descendant of Dion, has graciously furnished me with some exclusive details concerning the family. According to him, Samuel Smith Boursiquot separated from his wife in 1819. Shortly afterward he failed in his business and obtained a situation as gauger in the Excise. This sounds plausible, as a wholesale wine merchant would have received a proper training for that work. As gauger he went to Athlone, where he committed suicide by throwing himself out of the window of the hotel where he lived. There is also a legend of his being taken *flagrante delicto* and, escaping from an enraged husband, of meeting his death by jumping from the window of the bed-chamber.[4]

Although Boursiquot did eventually go to Athlone, much of the rest of Darley's information is either improbable or definitely erroneous. Boursiquot certainly remained in Dublin until at least 1829, for Tolson has found him still listed in *The Treble Almanack* as a wholesale merchant in the city until that date. Occasionally, Boursiquot shifted his place of business in Dublin, and his final business there, from 1827 to 1830, was 28, Bachelor's Walk. Dion himself confirms this address by referring in the introduction of his play *Robert Emmet* to "My father, S. Boucicault, of Bachelor's Walk, Dublin." In that same introduction, Dion gives one other slim clue to Boursiquot's character when he claims that his father was personally associated with Emmet, and "the house in which twenty years afterwards I was born, was, amongst others, searched for the fugitive rebel. . . ."

In a booklet titled *The Career of Dion Boucicault*, nominally written by the playwright's life-long friend Charles Lamb Kenney but ascribed by the playwright's third wife to Boucicault himself, there appears the information that Samuel Smith took his family to London in 1828, but when he failed in business a few years later returned to Dublin, leaving his sons in the care of his friend Lardner. Christopher Calthrop, Boucicault's great-grandson, has been able to establish the veracity of at least a part of the Kenney account:

> Certainly by August of 1829 Samuel Smith had moved his family to London because there exists a copy of a hand-written receipt signed by one of the Guinnesses of the Guinness, Mahon and Company bank of London which reads: "Mr. Boursiquot has handed me twenty pounds to be placed to credit of his account this 25th August 1829." A notation by the Dublin branch of the bank, dated 25 November 1831, speaks of him as "late of the City of London, merchant, now residing in the City of Florence," and another notation reveals that he was a resident of Athlone at least by 12 August 1839.[5]

The playwright himself mentions that his father "had a small place in Athlone and had obtained a managing clerkship in a distillery of an old friend, Robinson by name." [6] The rest of Darley's highly-colored account of Boursiquot's years in Athlone is highly suspect and has been partially refuted by Calthrop's discovery of Boursiquot's burial certificate, which states that the man was interred on April 11, 1853. Calthrop has also discovered a copy of Boursiquot's will, in which the man seems to have taken rather particular care to identify Dion as his legitimate son.

The case for Boursiquot's paternity rests on three points. First, he was married to Dion's mother. Second, Dion publicly referred to Boursiquot as his father and only referred to Lardner as his godfather and guardian. Third, there is no final and conclusive proof that Boursiquot was not Dion's father. The case for Lardner's paternity has, however, many persuasive points also.

First, from at least sometime in the summer of 1820, Mrs. Boursiquot seems incontestably to have been Lardner's mistress. The persistent Boucicault buff Christopher Calthrop has located in the House of Lords Record Office a copy of the Lardner divorce proceedings held in the Dublin Ecclesiastical Court, and the testimony of several witnesses indicates that at least in the summer and fall of 1820 Mrs. Boursiquot was Lardner's mistress. After his separation from his wife in October, 1820, Lardner resided for several months at 47, Lower Gardiner Street, the address traditionally accepted as Boucicault's birthplace. In the Lardner divorce proceedings, Mrs. Boursiquot remarks that she and her family moved to 28, Middle Gardiner Street in November, 1820. Second, the child was named after Lardner. Third, Lardner, despite financial obligations to his own children, did accept a responsibility for his namesake. In London, he acted openly as Dion's guardian, supporting him, paying for his schooling, and even allowing him a quarterly allowance after the boy ran away from school and went on the stage.

It is somewhat curious that Dion fairly often goes out of the way to stress the excellence of his paternal ancestry. Indeed, after his sojourn in Paris, he even affected a French title for awhile. This pride of family would seem to support his legitimacy, unless one thinks, as I am tempted to, that he doth protest too much.

Certain elements in the plot of *The Old Guard*, Boucicault's first play, which was written when he was still an impressionable schoolboy, seem provocatively autobiographical and pertinent. Henry Lefebre is the adopted son of Lord Beauville, and he falls in love with the girl his adopted father is attempting to seduce. He manages to thwart Lord Beauville, marry the girl, and come into an inheritance of a million francs. We doubtless could stretch the matter of the adopted son too far; yet it is interesting that Beauville is the villain of the piece and that Henry at the end

of the play is identified as the son and heir of the excellent
General Lefebre.

It would take little imagination to see this fable as a roman-
ticization of the young Boucicault's own situation. Certainly, it
fits in with his later romanticized pride of family and suggests a
youthful demand for legitimacy and an urgent reaction from his
tie, whatever its nature, with Lardner. It does not seem too
extreme to suggest that the young Boucicault resented his guardian in the same way that Henry resents Beauville. Dion's frequent
removals from school to school would suggest that he had an
unstable and unhappy childhood. He certainly escaped from
Lardner's protection as soon as he was able, and his own references to Lardner are dryly laconic.

About all that can be said is that the evidence concerning
Boucicault's paternity is contradictory and that none of it is
strong enough to be conclusive either way.

The question of when Boucicault was born is equally perplexing. On several occasions he himself quite clearly stated, "I
was born on the 26th of December, 1822." [7] However, The Dictionary of National Biography gives two other dates, December
26, 1820, and December 20, 1822. To complicate the matter,
Boucicault's mother in the London Times of February 2, 1842,
is reported as saying that he was born on December 7, 1820. [8]
And to complicate the matter even further, she is reported in the
previously mentioned records of the Dublin Ecclesiastical Court,
to have said that her son was born on December 27, 1820. [9]

There are, then, five different versions of Boucicault's birthdate, and just for the record one other theory should probably
be mentioned. Toward the end of his life, some of Boucicault's
acquaintances suggested that he was actually five or seven or
even ten years older than he admitted. According to this theory,
he might have been born anywhere from 1810 to 1817. There
seems, however, no factual evidence to support this view. Indeed,
Boucicault was the kind of individual to arouse gossip, and many
apocryphal stories—some of them outrageous—were told about
him at all stages of his career. It was even intimated that he
murdered his first wife by pushing her off a mountain in the
Alps. One of the qualities that gave rise to such stories is that he
was a bon vivant and ladies' man. The reports of his being five
to ten years older than he admitted were first heard around the

time, in 1885, when he entered into a December-June marriage with the ingenue of his company and neglected to go through the formality of divorce from the woman who for thirty years had been his publicly acknowledged wife. If Boucicault married young Louise Thorndyke when he was seventy-five or seventy, rather than sixty-five or sixty-three, it would make an enormously better story.

Several critics think it absurd to believe that Boucicault was only eighteen years old when he wrote *London Assurance,* a play that Krause has justly called "probably the best comedy since Farquhar." It would be, then, absurdity compounded to believe that the far from contemptible plays which preceded *London Assurance*—several of them professionally produced in the provinces—could have been written when Boucicault was fifteen to eighteen years old. Still, precocity does occur; and it would be easy to cite dozens of instances of it. Also, Boucicault was thrust when quite young into a rather interesting society; he did attend some of the more advanced schools of the day; and he was always noted for a quick, alert, ingenious, and fertile mind. That he wrote so well so young seems to me remarkable but not at all impossible.

Nevertheless, until more definite evidence of some sort appears, it remains as impossible to state exactly when Boucicault was born as it does to say exactly who was his father.

II *His Schooldays*

It is uncertain when Boucicault's schooldays began, but several reference books state that he was educated in part in Dublin, and Frank Dalton describes at some length Boucicault's boyish experiences in Dr. Geoghegan's Dublin academy.[10] Boucicault himself stated late in life that his first real awareness of himself and the world around him "was at a school in Hampstead in 1833, then a rural village three miles from London, now swallowed into the metropolis. It was a private school kept by Mr. Hessey, the father of the master of Merchant Tailors' School, and a dignitary of the Church." [11] This was a small school of only seven or eight boys, and in the same paragraph Boucicault mentions that he was ten years old when he was there. In the next paragraph, he mentions, "At fourteen I was removed from

Hessey's to the London University, but boarded in Euston
Square, near the school, with the Rev. Henry Stebbing, a most
amiable man and a historian of note." Boucicault's dates here
seem to be a bit off. Calthrop has established that the boy was
at University College School from 1833 to 1835. If he spent four
years at Mr. Hessey's, the years must have been from 1829 to
1833. Incidentally, Boucicault was not, as some writers have suggested, a university student; the University College School was
a grammar and secondary school for boys, which was founded
in 1830.

Boucicault also remarked that "in 1838 I found myself removed to a collegiate school in Brentford, kept by a Dr. Jamieson." Again, his date is wrong, for his actions in the spring and
fall of 1838 are quite definitely accounted for. Probably he meant
1837; if so, there is still a gap of about two years between his
stay at the University College School and his entrance at Brentford. There are several possibilities for these intervening years,
but the most likely is that he spent at least part of the time at
the famous Thomas Wright Hill School, at Bruce Castle, Totten-
ham, in North London. Several references, including the *Dictionary of National Biography* mention this school, and Calthrop
has discovered that Rowland Hill, at this time the moving spirit
of the school as well as the man responsible for England's adop-
tion of the penny postage, was a friend of Lardner.

There are two other possibilities for these years which should
at least be noted. Agnes Robertson, Boucicault's second wife,
mentioned that he went to school at Zion House, Margate;[12] and
Patrick Lynch and John Vaizey in their volume *Guinness's Brewery in the Irish Economy* mention that "One of the most interesting of the clerks was Dionysius Lardner Boursiquot . . . ,
the alleged son of a Dublin draper and of an ambitious mother
who kept a boarding house in Haddington Road. A personal
friend of some of the Guinnesses he left the brewery when he
was about eighteen, in 1840. . . ."

When queried by Calthrop, the authors could not recall where
they had run across these facts in the Guinness records, and in
reply to my own more recent queries the brewery now states
that Boucicault never worked there at all. Despite that dis-
claimer, I am not quite convinced and think it still possible that
Boucicault spent some time in Ireland, possibly in the summers,

and did work at the brewery. At any rate, it seems unlikely that
the Irish brogue which he retained all his life would have been
so strong had he not made frequent trips back to Ireland in his
boyhood. Also, Boucicault's mother's family was connected by
marriage to the Guinnesses. Although this connection may not
have been an unadulterated delight to the famous brewing family, it may still have helped young Boucicault to a temporary
clerkship during school vacations. Another even stronger possibility is that the possible brewery employment occurred after
Boucicault ran away from school and before he went on the
stage.

One fact is certain about Boucicault's schooldays: he was
often a rather poor scholar and often full of disruptive high
spirits. Still, he did attend some quite advanced schools; and a
great deal of knowledge did rub off on him, despite his frequent
position at the bottom of the class. Among other things, he got
the basis of his fluent French, which was to help him when he
made his later piratical raids on Parisian drama. Really, Boucicault seemed to take a pragmatic view of knowledge. He
skimmed over a large territory and filed away in his mind those
areas which he might some day put to use. To give a few symptomatic instances of his learning, I might note that he was always able to drop a Latin tag, that he could creditably discuss
Aristotle's theory of the drama, that he could find his way sure-
footedly through the major English drama critics from Dryden
to his own day, and, indeed, that he had a wide knowledge of
English literature, particularly the drama. His knowledge of most
topics unconnected with the stage was probably wider and less
deep, but John Coleman was not wildly exaggerating in writing
that "He knew something about everything. . . ." [13]

III   *Early Days on the Stage*

Boucicault's first delighted experience of the stage was at
Brentford, when he became involved in a school production of
Pizarro, Richard Brinsley Sheridan's adaptation of Kotzebue's
The Spaniards in Peru. Boucicault wrote: "The part of Rolla fell
to me, and then, for the first time, my mind seemed to soar. I
wanted to play every part in the piece, but had to content myself by teaching all the rest how their parts should be given.

I never controlled so obedient and enthusiastic a crowd." [14] He also wrote an afterpiece for the occasion called *The Old Guard*, a play which was produced several years later in London and New York, and which managed to hold the boards for some years.

Shortly after the production of this first play, Boucicault left Brentford. He may at this time have returned to Dublin and worked at the Guinness Brewery for a short while, but it was not long before he was in London apprenticed to Dr. Lardner as a civil engineer. According to family tradition, as Walsh notes, Boucicault helped lay the first railway line from London to Harrow; and this work would certainly fit in with what we know of Lardner's own activity after resigning his chair at London University.

It was probably in the spring of 1838 that Boucicault turned to the professional stage. It may have been his delight in the theater, his irritation with civil engineering, his dislike of Lardner, or a combination of all three that impelled him. At any rate, he took the name of Lee Moreton and made his way to Gloucestershire, where Charles Hill was managing the Cheltenham and Gloucester theaters. He pestered Hill to give him a trial as an actor and an engagement if he was successful. Hill gave him the role of Tressel in *Richard III*, and apparently Boucicault was quite successful, for his next appearance was in the famous part of Sir Giles Overreach in Philip Massinger's *A New Way to Pay Old Debts*.

Lardner was still maintaining his responsibility for the boy. Barton Hill, Charles Hill's son, later recalled that his father, having taken Boucicault under his wing, "thus came into correspondence for some few years with this young man's guardians, legal advisers of the celebrated scientist and writer, Dr. Dionysius Lardner. . . ." [15]

In the spring of 1838, Hill leased the Theatre Royal in Brighton; and in June Boucicault traveled with the Hills to Brighton, where Hill opened the theater on July 21. Boucicault's first Brighton appearance was on July 30, again as Sir Giles; and a reviewer remarked of his performance:

He labours under the disadvantage of a bad stage voice. [16] We know not what time may do for him, but now his voice certainly wants that depth of tone so essential to dramatic representation. He is a young man of promise, though his first appearance certainly presented us with many of those defects which are almost inseparable from so young an actor. Some of the speeches were spoken with rather over-studied effect, and the gentleman has a constant bad habit of stooping at making points.[17]

At Brighton, Boucicault got his first real taste of provincial repertory—acting at night while working up a new part during the day. In quick succession, he appeared in several new roles. Apparently, Hill decided to capitalize on the boy's brogue, for most of Boucicault's parts were Irish ones. On August 10, he played the lead role of Tom Moore, an Irish tailor, in a farce called *The Irish Lion;* on August 17, he acted the Irish role of Larry O'Gig in a play called *The Robber's Wife;* on August 23, he took the leading role of Murtoch Delany in *The Irishman in London;* on August 25, he played Osric in *Hamlet;* on August 30, he played the title role, an Irish one, in the farce of *Teddy the Tiler;* on September 21, he took the title role in Samuel Lover's *Rory O'More,* and at the end of the first act he danced an Irish jig creditably with Mrs. Hill.

Busy as he was, he also found time to write. On October 1, he played the minor comic part of Teddy Rodent, an Irish rat catcher, in his own melodrama, *A Legend of the Devil's Dyke.* The piece is a farrago of melodramatic claptrap, but notable for the semblance of realism and local color around Brighton.

Having gained some experience, Boucicault was apparently ready to try his wings, and so he returned alone to Cheltenham where he appeared at the Theatre Royal for two weeks in December, playing some of his usual roles and several new ones, including Grady O'Shaugnessy in a musical farce *The £100 Note,* Backbite in Richard Brinsley Sheridan's *The School for Scandal,* and Gerald Pepper in Lover's *The White Horse of the Peppers.* In 1839 he also played in Bristol and Hull, and on March 9 he made his London debut both as an actor and a playwright, when a farcical one-act called *Lodgings to Let* was produced at the Haymarket. On May 6, the playlet was repeated at the Strand Theatre in London.

On December 28, 1839, his dramatization of Harrison Ainsworth's novel *Jack Sheppard* was produced at Hull and other

towns. Years later Boucicault remarked to Charles Reade and
John Coleman that he had played it at Leeds, which he described as:

"A one-horse shay place. Anyhow, it was so when I was leading
actor in the York circuit."

"I didn't know you were ever a leading actor."

"Ever, sir! I was the original Jack Sheppard in your beastly hole
of a theatre."

"Tate Wilkinson thought it charming."

"Ah! that was a hundred years ago, and a good deal of water
has flowed under Leeds bridge since then. Well, I hope you'll
have better luck with 'It's never too late to mend' than I had with
Jack Sheppard, for I came a cropper of twenty feet from the flies,
and nearly broke every bone in my body in the escape from New-
gate."

"Indeed!"

"Yes; I thought I'd got my quietus. They had to drop the curtain, and Leigh Murray took my part, while his (Thames Darrell)
was taken by Bob Roxby. That was my last appearance in Leeds."

"And your last as a leading actor, I suppose?"

"Oh dear no! I opened immediately after at Brighton as Sir
Giles Overreach."

The idea of Boucicault, with that accent, appearing as Sir Giles
tickled Reade's fancy so much that he roared.

"Did you make Sir Giles an Irishman, Dion?"

"Did the devil! No, sir; I made him a great tragic part!" [18]

During 1840, Boucicault appears to have given up acting and
to have spent much of his time in London. In March, Lardner
eloped with Mrs. Heaviside; and we may assume that his allowance to Boucicault came to an end. It is probably at this time
that Mrs. Boursiquot may have persuaded Arthur Lee Guinness
of the famous brewery, and a family connection, to take an interest in her son, who seemed now without prospects of any
kind. As Agnes Robertson, Boucicault's second wife, later remarked:

About this time Arthur Lee Guinness, a cousin of Mrs. Boucicault,
proposed to adopt Boucicault and leave him fortune, and on the
strength of this Boucicault commenced his London career, though
in a very different way from what Mr. Guinness had intended.

Instead of diligently pursuing his collegiate studies he started a cab and a "tiger," lived at Long's Hotel, and gave generous suppers to his literary friends; in fact it may be said that his course of life did not accord with Mr. Guinness' ideas of intellectual progress. So one morning Boucicault received a letter from his patron saying that as he had not followed his advice he might consider himself cut off from the promised fortune.[19]

Agnes's account sounds as if her husband had touched it up a bit in relating it to her, but the broad outlines certainly accord with Dion's later penchant for high living and also with the gay, spendthrift young dogs who were the heroes of some of his early comedies.

With the loss of all of his prospects, Boucicault was thrown back on his writing and had for some months a difficult time of it in London. Late in life, he painted a rather romantic picture of himself in his London garret:

I was eighteen years of age at that time. I am sixty-six now. Forty-eight years ago! *Eheu! fugaces labuntur anni!* Ah me!—where was I?

Follow me down a narrow street leading from the Strand to the river: Villiers Street, I think it was called, but it has been improved out of the map of London to make room for the Charing-Cross Railway Station. Let us enter a dingy lodging-house and mount four flights of dark and greasy stairs. The door facing the visitors is that of the back attic, or rather the back garret, for the room is nestled in the roof of the building and receives its light from a dormer-window. It is small; so is its rent—four shillings a week. The furniture consists of a low iron bedstead, two wicked-looking chairs, and a washstand; there are neither curtains nor carpet; a plain substantial table, covered with manuscripts and writing material, stands near the window. The mantelpiece accommodates a row of books, consisting of prizes won at school, in their showy bindings; a score of French novels, ragged and disreputable as their contents; a copy of Voltaire's Philosophical Dictionary; a Shakespeare and a collection of Cumberland's London stage, flanked by an earthenware pot of tea and a monstrous teacup.

Leaning at the open window, contemplating the vista of chimney-pots and disconsolate tiled roofs that spread away to the smoky horizon of Lambeth; sat the lodger in this Bohemian asylum. He was something older than a boy and younger than a man.

His slim figure, broad in the shoulders, thin in the flank; his black hair and gray-blue eyes; his complexion, as fair as that of a girl, indicates the Irish race.[20]

He also remarked that he was "drifting from one poor lodging to another, selling the little I had to obtain the means of life, cleansing my own shoes, but refusing to return to my father's house in Dublin, and confess to being the prodigal I am (and have always been)." Two of his brothers, he said, had by this time emigrated to Australia; and his mother lived with his eldest brother, a clerk in a Dublin bank. His father, he wrote, "was very aged and infirm. There was no room for me at home excepting in my mother's heart, so I stayed away."

IV Success as a Playwright

During 1840, Boucicault was doing considerable writing and hoping desperately to improve his fortunes by placing one of his plays with a London manager. This world of the Victorian theater, at whose door Boucicault was knocking, was in a slow state of transition. There were still "major" and "minor" houses, and Covent Garden and Drury Lane would not lose their patents and their sole privilege of producing the legitimate drama until 1843. Polite society rarely patronized the theater, and the audience was largely composed of the lower and middle classes who avidly sought entertainment. To a large extent, this entertainment-seeking audience determined the Victorian theater. Great barns of theaters were built to accommodate the mass audience, and actors broadened their styles to reach out to the faraway gallery. The bill was lengthened to four or five or even six hours, and might include a main piece, a curtain-raising farce, and a closing burletta. Although good plays were certainly written, there was an overwhelming demand for broad comedy, exciting melodrama, and extravaganzas with spectacular effects. In this world, the place of the playright was, as George Rowell described it, "that of handyman to the company. He existed to make their performance possible, rather than they to interpret his work to an audience."[21] It was not a world in which the art of the drama could flourish.

For that reason, Boucicault was extremely lucky in placing *London Assurance* with one of the few companies from which he could get a sensitive production. In November, he submitted his one-act farce *A Lover by Proxy* to Charles Mathews and Madame Vestris at the Covent Garden Theatre, using his pseudonym of Lee Moreton. According to Boucicault's later account, Mathews had merely glanced at the title page and thought that the piece was by the established dramatist Maddison Morton. Impressed by the piece, Mathews called "Morton" into his office to discuss it and was shocked to find that the real author was only a boy who had not yet reached his eighteenth birthday. Boucicault later drew an affecting, if perhaps heightened, picture of how he broke down and cried at Mathews' kindness. At any rate, Mathews refused this Regency farce; but he put Boucicault on the free list of the theater and remarked: "I wish I could help you, but we are glutted with farces. What we do want now-a-days is a good five-act comedy of modern life." Four weeks later, the indefatigable Boucicault returned with the script of *London Assurance,* which was accepted; it was shortly put into rehearsal, during which it received rigorous revisions, and was produced on March 4, 1841.

The play had a brilliant cast and was a resounding success. Part of its acclaim was doubtless due to the superb acting of Mathews in the role of Dazzle, and part to the elaborately realistic box sets which utilized a dazzling array of real carpets, furniture, chandeliers, and looking glasses. The painstakingly realistic setting of the piece was an attractive novelty and predated the realism of Tom Robertson by a quarter of a century. Still, despite the brilliance of the acting and the novelty of the setting, the piece had its own very real merit. It continued to be a favorite throughout the nineteenth century and was as successful with mediocre casts as it was with brilliant ones.

Boucicault received £300 for the play; and, excited by his heady success, he brought his mother and elder brother to stay with him in London. "They consented to join him in London for a visit of six months," he remarked years later. "They remained forty years." [22]

He discovered quite quickly that the brilliant success of *London Assurance* was no assurance at all that London had taken

him to its heart. Indeed, as he was to discover, the success of
a really good play in the Victorian theater was something of a
fluke. Nevertheless, he had now not only to support his mother
and brother but also his own extravagant way of life. Throughout his career, he made a fantastic amount of money, but he
spent it on theatrical ventures and on high living just about as
quickly as he made it. This constant and pressing need for more
money, as well as the lowbrow milieu of the London stage, con-
tributed largely to his own artistic disintegration.

After *London Assurance*, Boucicault very quickly turned out
a large number of plays. As he later stated, "the race-horse went
to the plow with a little sigh, as he put his neck in the collar to
work for weekly wages. Sometimes he took a free gallop, as
when he wrote 'The School for Scheming', and 'Love in a Maze';
but these five-act comedies added more to his literary merit than
to his pecuniary credit." [23] In 1842, five plays by Boucicault appeared in London; in 1843, there were three more plays; in 1844,
there were seven; in 1845, there were two; in 1846, there were
five.

There was considerable range in these pieces. *The Irish Heiress* of 1842 was a respectable comedy, and *Old Heads and Young
Hearts* of 1844 is probably an even better piece than *London
Assurance*. The rest ranged from trivial farces and conventional
melodramas to translations and adaptations from the French, hasty
collaborations, and revisions of early work. Easy money rather
than difficult labor was often his chief motive. As he later remarked:

> I was a beginner in 1841, and received for my comedy "London
> Assurance," £300. For that amount the manager bought the privi-
> lege of playing the work for the season. Three years later I offered
> a new play to a principal London Theatre. The manager offered
> me £100 for it. In reply to my objection to the smallness of the
> sum he remarked, "I can go to Paris and select a first-class comedy;
> having seen it performed, I feel certain of its effect. To get this
> comedy translated will cost me £25. Why should I give you
> £300 or £500 for your comedy of the success of which I cannot
> feel so assured?" The argument was unanswerable and the result
> inevitable, I sold a work for £100 that took me six months' hard
> work to compose, and accepted a commission to translate three

French pieces at £50 a piece. This work afforded me child's play for a fortnight. Thus the English dramatist was obliged to relinquish the stage altogether or to become a French copyist.[24]

To give him his due, Boucicault did try to write as well as he could. Ultimately, however, the Victorian theater won out. No one man, no matter how talented, could change overnight the taste of the audience and the practice of the managers—and Boucicault was only a very young man. That change in taste was a slow process of evolution. Twenty-five years later, the fine writer Tom Robertson could make only a little more headway, and at the end of the century even the serious parts of Oscar Wilde's plays were still quite conventional. Yet, in the last analysis, the efforts of all of these men and a few others, like Bulwer-Lytton and Charles Reade in their best work, had an effect. So when Bernard Shaw appeared in the 1890's as a John the Baptist for Henrik Ibsen (but really for himself), the ground had already been prepared. Boucicault and Robertson and others had made it ready. Still, there were casualties, and Boucicault was one of them. As we shall see, he exerted great effect in many ways on the Victorian stage, but the Victorian stage had its own degenerating effect on him.

On July 9, 1845, Boucicault married a French widow, Anne Guiot, who was the daughter of Etienne St. Pierre. The marriage took place in the parish church of St. Mary, Lambeth, London. Little is known of Anne or of the marriage. Tolson speculates that the couple left for the Continent after the production at the Lyceum on August 25 of Dion's one-act farce *Enquire Within*. Stephen Fiske, a journalist who was obviously repeating gossip, wrote: "They took a tour through Switzerland. Boucicault went up the Alps with a wife, and came down with a black hatband. How did the wife die? Nobody knows; but Boucicault must have inherited her money, for he returned to London and drove a pair of gray ponies in Hyde Park, and resumed his semi-fashionable, semi-Bohemian life." [25]

It is more probable that Anne did not immediately die, for Boucicault spent about four years in France, during which time he apparently familiarized himself with the Parisian stage. However, during his bankruptcy proceedings in 1848, he mentioned that his wife had left him more than £1000. He also mentioned, somewhat romantically, that he was an Irishman but the son of a Frenchman, that his name was de Bourcicault, and that, when he lived in France, he had used his rightful title of Viscount de Bourcicault.

Back in England and, as usual, hard-pressed for cash, Boucicault continued his prolific hack work for the stage. By this time it was only the occasional play that contained any sign of his more than casual attention. Still, he had solidified his reputation as a competent journeyman playwright; and, when Charles Kean became the lessee of the Princess Theater in 1850, he hired Boucicault as his literary adviser for the sum of £700 a year.

Most of Boucicault's plays at this time were hasty adaptations, but some were attractive melodramatic vehicles for a leading actor—especially *Sixtus V, The Corsican Brothers,* and *Louis XI.* The last two were among the most successful in Kean's repertoire, and Henry Irving later found the title roles admirably suited to his own peculiar talents. *The Vampire* (later revised and titled *The Phantom*), which was produced at the Princess on June 14, 1852, is worth mentioning, although hardly for its own claptrap merits. This pre-Bela Lugosi thriller is notable for being the first professional play in which Boucicault acted under his own name, and it was also his first appearance on the boards since his early days in the provinces. Walsh, following the account of Henry Morley, records that "Boucicault enacted the 'monster' with due paleness of visage, stealthiness of pace and solemnity of tone"—and also with a broad Irish brogue.

Boucicault's connection with Kean introduced him to Agnes Robertson, a young Scottish actress who was the protégée and ward of the Keans, and who was to be Boucicault's faithful partner for many years, both on the stage and off. The daughter of Thomas Robertson of Edinburgh, she was born on Christmas Day, 1833. She made her first appearance on the stage at the age of ten at the Theatre Royal, Aberdeen, and continued to act in the provinces until her London debut at the Princess in *The Wife's Secret* on October 16, 1850.

There is no record of when and where Boucicault married Agnes, and in the last years of his life he both admitted the marriage and denied it. If we are to believe Boucicault that his mother opposed his return to acting until she learned that he had married an actress, then the marriage must have occurred before the production of *The Vampire*. At any rate, Boucicault wrote for Agnes the sentimental drama called *The Prima Donna* in which she appeared at the Princess and often later with considerable success.

V *Agnes (and Dion) in America*

After some disagreement with Kean (". . . Kayne—I mayne Kean—was about to throw me over," Boucicault later remarked to John Coleman), Boucicault left his employ. Early in August, 1853, Agnes sailed for New York, and on September 19 filled an engagement in Montreal. Dion himself had arrived in New York on the previous day, September 18. As her mentor and manager, he immediately introduced her to the boards in New York and shortly later in Boston, where she scored a resounding personal success which she was to enjoy on American stages for several years.

This first American reaction to Agnes' acting is vividly described in the blurb on the inside front cover of the Samuel French edition of Dion's *Andy Blake; or, The Irish Diamond:*

> After a career of three months in New York, where she had gathered around her a host of admirers, she went to Boston in January, 1854, and made her celebrated *debut* at the Boston Museum. The excitement caused by her performances spread throughout the city and environs; it gained the neighboring villages, towns and cities, and special trains were run to bring thousands to witness this exquisite actress. The engagement was prolonged from two to four weeks, then to six, and subsequently to eight weeks. By this time the furore had become beyond all precedent. The tickets of admission were sold at a premium of five and six dollars each, and at her benefit, the last night of her engagement, the applicants for seats blocked up the access to the theatre and the street in front. The manager, Mr. Moses Kimball, induced Miss Robertson to prolong her performances for the ninth week, and within four hours, such was the crowd that every seat in the theatre was bought up for the ensuing week. Such was the enthusiasm created by Miss Robertson amongst the ladies of Boston, that her promenades through the streets were beset with crowds who followed her from place to place. The corridors of the Tremont House, where she resided, were blocked up with fair admirers,

who fairly invaded her apartments. The childlike grace, and sweetness of manner, with which she received all these honors, that fell so suddenly and thickly upon her, won more hearts to her cause than the exquisite power of her acting on the stage. During this engagement . . . Mr. Kimball, the manager, netted something like twenty thousand dollars. . . .

Nothing is more difficult than the attempt to recapture, from old press notices and reviews, the quality that made a player from the past so impressive. However, there are many accounts of "The Fairy Star," as Agnes was called in these years; and from them we can gather considerable information about the scope, if not the actual vitality, of her talent. She was a beautiful little woman, and she still had a very youthful appearance on the stage. She could dance, she could sing, she was a splendid mimic, and she could take off a boy's part superlatively, as is shown by her continued success as Bob Nettles in Tom Taylor's *To Parents and Children* and in the title role of Dion's *Andy Blake.* An indication of her range, if not her verve and charm, can be seen in this résumé of a typical vehicle play which Dion wrote for her, *The Young Actress:*

Mr. Crosschex, a theatrical manager, finds himself in awkward position when his company refuses to act the evening of his benefit unless he pays the salaries he owes them and doubles their wages. He is unable to meet their demands and is in quite a temper. As he is explaining the circumstances to his wife, who is impressed only by the beautiful contours of his head, his daughter, Maria, enters and informs him that she has decided to become an actress. He forbids her to go on the stage, and in the midst of his admonitions, a call-boy announces a deputation of the rebellious actors. Maria insists that her father receive them and depend upon her for a solution of his problem.

Various players call upon Crosschex in search of employment while he converses with the representatives of his company of actors and listens to their demands. The members of the deputation, who have heard Mrs. Crosschex announce that a new company has arrived, begin to feel that their position is no longer secure. They succumb to Crosschex' conditions after they have heard a number of these actors, who hail from Yorkshire, Germany and Ireland. Maria then enters and informs her father that she had impersonated the various roles. His objections to her embracing the theatrical profession are thus overcome and the curtain drops.[26]

A clever idea, although not, incidentally, original with Boucicault, for he was closely following Edward Lancaster's play *The Manager's Daughter.* Obviously, however, this piece stands or falls on the ability of the actress playing Maria to take off a number of different types, and apparently Agnes could do it consummately.

In another of these vehicle plays, Boucicault's *The Fairy Star,* which was first presented on November 6, 1854, Agnes played five different roles as well as sang and danced in the *Killicranke Broadsword Lilt,* the *Lebe Vohl,* the *Ric-ty-a,* an Irish jig, and the English Middy's song, *The Bay of Cronstadt Oh!* Although her forte was comedy, she was also adept at the straight sentimental role, many of which she filled with more than adequacy.

At first, Dion himself stayed in the background, giving only some mildly received lectures in New York and Boston, managing his wife's career, and continuing his own writing. Much of his writing from 1853 until late in 1857 consisted of vehicles to exploit Agnes' talents. For her, he scribbled such theatrically successful ephemera as the already mentioned *The Young Actress, Andy Blake,* and *The Fairy Star,* as well as *Agnes Robertson at Home, The Cat Changed into a Woman,* and *Rachel Is Coming.*

It is impossible not to admire Agnes, for she had with Boucicault a rigorous life. During these American years, they were almost constantly on the move, playing in all of the major towns on the eastern seaboard, as far into the Middle West as Chicago and St. Louis, and as far south as New Orleans. Dion had, of course, times of really plush prosperity; but he and Agnes spent much time on trains and in cheap boarding houses. Just how much of a trouper she was can be seen by the fact that she bore him six children with only brief respites from her appearances on the stage. Their oldest, Dion William, was born on May 10, 1855, in New Orleans; Eve, on October 10, 1857, in New York; Darley George, on May 23, 1859, in New York; Patrice, on August 9, 1862, in London; Nina, on February 27, 1867, in London; and their last, Aubrey Robertson, on June 23, 1869.

Certainly, Boucicault was not the easiest person to live with.

He was charming, but he was a very busy man, he was convivial, and he had a wandering eye. And, as a producer, he dropped the role of loving husband entirely. Here, for example, is an anecdote related of the Boucicaults in rehearsal in 1858, by J. B. Howe, an actor in the company:

. . . let me relate an instance of the thorough business instinct and professional impartiality of one whom I consider the greatest writer and adaptor of modern drama in the world, and one of the finest character actors on the stage. On the morning of the rehearsal of "The Life of an Actress," Miss Agnes Robertson failed to do a little bit of business of kneeling and falling at the feet of the gentleman who played the heavy part, and Dion asked her to do it again. Agnes did it again, but in the same manner as before.

"No, no; that won't do," said Dion. "Can't you rise slowly from your chair, giving the audience the idea that you are still under the influence of the narcotic? Grasp the corner of the table, so, and, as if fearing to fall, you still retain your hold on the table until your left knee touches the ground; then is the time to seize Mr. Ralston's right hand with your left, so, and you turn gently round and fall in the centre at his feet."

"I know that, Dion dear, but is there any necessity for me to do all that now? I've played the part before."

"I know that, but not with the present members. I want *them* to see what you are going to do; go back, please. Please, Mr. Ralston, once more, to oblige Mrs. Boucicault. Now, if you please."

But the sweet little creature did not please. She burst into tears, and Dion exclaimed, "Never mind, ladies and gentlemen; dismiss the rehearsal." That was all; we dispersed, and, need I say, in the most elegant confusion.[27]

VI *On Tour*

The second half of Boucicault's life was a time of intense, varied, and almost unceasing theatrical activity. He became one of the most prolific writers, the most admired actors, and the most successful managers of the last half of the nineteenth century. He played all of the major and many of the minor cities in the United States, England, Ireland, and Australia. It is impossible to estimate closely the innumerable performances of his many plays, and just as impossible to judge how much money he made and spent. At one moment he lived, as Coleman put it, *"en grand seigneur"* at the Countess of Blessington's former mansion at Kensington Gore; at another time, he owned his own yacht; at another, he was bankrupt.

Still, perhaps only the most notable events need be recounted, for the many incidents of his later life had all of the thrilling excitement and monotonous similarity that inevitably attaches to a life in the theater.

On September 22, 1854, he made his American acting debut in Boston as Sir Patrick O'Plenipo in *The Irish Artist*. On November 10, he made his New York debut as Sir Charles Coldstream in his own very popular play, *Used Up*. After this engagement, he acted constantly with Agnes, and his popularity soon equalled hers. He developed into a character actor of great power; and, even toward the end of his acting career when he was in his sixties, he could still play his dashing Irish roles with a convincingly youthful appearance and a vivid gusto. He fancied himself adept in tragedy, but his real forte was pathos and melodrama and, above all, comedy. This insistence that he could act tragedy was probably his one blind spot of egotism as an actor, but he wisely kept overwhelmingly to the roles that he could do. Once, however, he essayed the title role in his *Louis XI*, and the results were disastrous:

At first the audience sat in dumb amazement; then came titters and giggles, and finally roars. Never did monarch receive less grave and reverent treatment. Boucicault's brogue came out thick and strong. . . . As the tragedy—or, more properly speaking, the tragic farce—progressed, John Brougham, who loved a good joke better than anything else in the world, began to exaggerate the unctuousness of his own fine, natural brogue. Next John Clayton, an Englishman and the son-in-law of Boucicault, who was playing *Nemours*, felt in duty bound to fall in with the others, and he too assumed a broad brogue. The rest of the company, either out of deviltry or catching the infection, became Gaelic instead of Gallic, and before the play was half over the French tragedy had degenerated into an orgy of Hibernian dialects. . . . People laughed till the tears ran down their cheeks.[28]

Wisely, Boucicault never repeated the experiment.

In 1855, the Boucicaults toured the eastern and middle-western states, and in December Dion took over the management of

the Gaiety Theatre in New Orleans. The venture was not a success, and after about three months Boucicault gave it up. On
August 18, 1856, Congress passed a copyright law, largely as a
result of agitation by Boucicault and George Henry Boker. After
another year of touring, Boucicault and William Stuart opened
the Washington Theatre in the nation's capital. Again, the venture was not a success; but in 1859 Boucicault and Stuart thoroughly renovated the old Metropolitan Theatre in New York,
rechristened it the Winter Garden, and opened on September 14
with *Dot*, Boucicault's dramatization of *The Cricket on the
Hearth*.

On December 6, the Winter Garden saw the *première* of Boucicault's *The Octoroon; or, Life in Louisiana*. This play about
the South and the slavery question was an instant success, but
Agnes and Dion shortly withdrew from the cast after an argument over their salaries. They moved to Laura Keene's Theatre
in New York, opening on January 9, 1860, with *Jeanie Deans*,
an adaptation of Scott's *The Heart of Mid-Lothian*. This successful piece was followed on March 12 by *Vanity Fair*, which was
not an adaptation from Thackeray and which failed. To provide
a piece to keep the theater open, Dion dashed out a very free
adaptation of Gerald Griffin's novel *The Collegians*. This Irish
play, *The Colleen Bawn*, opened on March 29, was hugely successful, and inaugurated a rash of imitations.

In July, the Boucicaults sailed for England, and on September
10 they opened at the Adelphi Theatre, London, in *The Colleen
Bawn*. The play proved as successful in London and ran for 278
performances, at that time a record. Queen Victoria saw the play
three times. In April, 1861, the Boucicaults played the piece for
twenty-four nights in Dublin to packed houses. This triumphant
return must have been a considerable satisfaction to Dion.

Boucicault made a very great deal of money from *The Colleen
Bawn*, and he promptly lost it all in an attempt to renovate
Astley's old Amphitheatre into a modern one which he called
The Theatre Royal, Westminster. This project was an extremely
expensive one which included such non-theatrical enticements
as walks, gardens, and roof gardens. However, the theater was
in a seedy portion of London, and Boucicault found it impossible
to entice enough patrons. Finally, on June 12, 1863, the enter-

prise collapsed; and Boucicault, now bankrupt, left for the provinces to recoup his fortunes.

His first ploy was to exhume an adaptation of his which he had presented in America in 1857 under the title of *The Poor of New York*. With a few localizing touches and a change of title to *The Poor of Liverpool*, the old play proved to have some fire still in it. Actually, it had quite a bit of fire, particularly in the sensation scene of the burning tenement. Boucicault returned to London with the play, now called *The Streets of London*, and demanded not a flat royalty per night but an unprecedented share of the profits. He succeeded in getting what he wanted, and the play was so popular that he was soon on his feet again.

Boucicault's notable work for 1864 was the first version of *Arrah-na-Pogue; or, The Wicklow Wedding*, which he originally produced at the old Theatre Royal in Dublin on November 7. However, this version was considerably different from the play as we know it today, and Boucicault's reminiscence of how he tinkered with it offers an instructive glimpse into what a canny purveyor of entertainment he had become:

> "All's well that ends well," but, be jabers! poor "Arrah" had a near squeak for her life in Dublin. I'd devised a kind of Irish Meg Merrilees for Sam Emery which nearly cooked the piece and sent it to blazes. Then there was a little comedy part for Sam Johnson which was no use and it had to go too. In fact I had to put the back where the belly was, and the belly on the back, and turn the whole thing inside out. But I saw the strength as well as the weakness: I've nailed the one and knifed the other.
>
> Even then the play wouldn't have been what it is if it hadn't been for Vining. When I read it to him, he said, "Right as rain!— save that it wants a fillip to the last act. By Jove!" he burst out, "I've got it!—got it in the Theatre too! Do you remember that wretched 'Golden Daggers' thing that Ned Yates did for Harris and Fechter? Well, we've got the three sinking bridges (cost five or six hundred pounds and only used for a week) here!—here under our feet! I'll go and see Lloyd this moment and arrange to work 'em into your escape. This effect and a song for Arrah, and there you are, my boy!" [29]

Indeed, he was, for the play ran 164 performances at the Princess Theatre in London. Later in 1865, on September 4, the

American actor Joe Jefferson opened at the Adelphi in London with the final version of *Rip Van Winkle,* which Boucicault had assembled for him from an earlier lackluster version; the piece ran for 170 performances and became the most famous role in Jefferson's repertoire.

From 1866 to 1872 Boucicault was both prosperous and extremely busy. Play after play came from his pen. However, most of them were in some degree adaptations and showed little more merit than the slick craftsmanship of a very canny theatrical hack. In the plays of these years, Boucicault shamelessly pandered to popular taste. However, *Hunted Down* of 1866 was notable for giving Henry Irving his London debut. In the same year, *Flying Scud,* Boucicault's horse-racing melodrama, achieved a London run of 207 performances. *After Dark, Formosa,* and *Lost at Sea* were all sensational melodramas of little or no literary merit. Boucicault's total surrender to popular entertainment may be gauged by comparing *The Rapparee* of 1870 to *The Colleen Bawn* or *Arrah-na-Pogue.* The earlier Irish plays were entertainments, but there was some valid observation in them and some solid craftsmanship. The new Irish play was nothing but a farrago of thrills, sensation scenes, and stock sentiment.

In 1872, Boucicault was asked to write a play by the Earl of Londsborough; and he conceived, as Walsh put it, "the idea of a colossal spectacle which should eclipse anything ever before attempted within the four walls of a theatre." What emerged was an extravaganza, written by Boucicault and J. R. Planché, called *Babil and Bijou,* which opened at Covent Garden on August 29. As Walsh described it,

> An army of men, women and children took part. There were dancers, comedians, pantomimists, Amazonian warriors and coryphees galore, together with a huge fantastic aquarium of pseudo oysters, crabs, cockles, seals, periwinkles, sea-lions, sea-horses, sharks, alligators, sword-fish, devil-fish and lobsters—scarlet boiled lobsters at that!—at the bottom of the ocean (possibly it was the Red Sea).
>
> The action transpired in every conceivable realm, from mid-air to the bowels of the earth. . . .[30]

All reports of the production indicate that it was a charming and visually fantastic spectacle. However, Boucicault went about the production in the same grandiose manner that had scuttled some of his previous enterprises, such as the Winter Garden and The Theatre Royal, Westminster. The play cost £11,000 to mount, a huge sum in those days; and no matter how long it ran, it could not recover its continuing production costs.

Early in September, Boucicault and Agnes sailed for New York. Boucicault has sometimes been accused of running away from the Covent Garden fiasco, but the truth seems to be that he had already planned to return to New York. Agnes played a few engagements with him, but the Fairy Star had begun to dim. Agnes had already been on the stage for about thirty years, and she was a middle-aged woman now. She was no longer as convincing in some of her early parts, and she soon returned to London.

Alone, Dion formed a traveling company and added several new plays to his repertoire, most of them, however, adaptations and none of them of great merit. In January, 1874, the company arrived in San Francisco from Canada; and, after an engagement there, slowly began to make its way back east, stopping in many places including Virginia City, where the young David Belasco briefly acted as Dion's amanuensis.

The best play of these years was Boucicault's superb Irish drama *The Shaughraun,* which opened at Wallack's Theatre in New York on November 14, and grossed $220,076.50 during its run. Dion found in Conn the Shaughraun probably his most memorable role, and the fifty-two-year-old actor entered into the taxing eighteen-year-old part with a totally convincing verve. He was, as Walsh put it,

> . . . obliged to jump in and out of cabin windows, to scale prison walls that revolved in full view of the audience . . . , to climb over abbey ruins and execute a "back fall" down a precipitous "run"; after being "stretched out" and "waked" as a genuine corpse, to come to life for a hand-to-hand encounter with a pair of ruffians. . . . These and numerous other exploits of *Conn* might have taxed the physical resources of a younger man than Boucicault, but the veteran romped through the play like a two-year old colt, with unquenchable gusto.[31]

In September, 1875, Dion and Agnes opened in London in *The Shaughraun;* but the quite successful run was blighted on the last night by news of the death of their eldest son in a railroad accident.

In 1876, Boucicault was again in America, and his droll farce *Forbidden Fruit* was produced at Wallack's on October 3. However, as Tolson justly notes, "Boucicault was not writing as rapidly as had been his practice. From the very nature of the plays produced during the period between *The Shaughraun* and the date of his death, it appears that he had lost his touch. And then again, it is also true that the wants of the theater-going public had changed. Boucicault had not kept apace with his public; he had either failed to keep his hand on its pulse, or, feeling the heart's action, had been unable to supply its demands." [32]

VII *Last Years*

He was still active. Indeed, his continuing activities as writer, actor, and manager might have worn out a younger man. There were still new plays, but not many of them are worth notice. In 1877 and 1878 he toured and played often in New York. In February, 1879 Agnes briefly joined him in New York for a revival of *The Colleen Bawn.* In the middle of March, he himself was in England reviving *Formosa* at Drury Lane; in September, he was producing a new piece in New York. However, he was beginning to tire; and the winter of 1879/80 saw him laid up for three months. In February, though, he was playing at Wallack's; and in April he revived *The Shaughraun* at the Adelphi in London. In August he played in *The Bridal Tour* at the Haymarket; and in October he opened in *The O'Dowd* at the Adelphi.

Early in 1883 he was again in New York with a new company, playing, among other pieces, his new Irish play, *The Amadan,* with his son Dion, Jr., in the cast. In May, Agnes again appeared briefly with him in New York in *The Colleen Bawn.* His only new play in 1884 was *Robert Emmet,* which he opened in Chicago with Dion, Jr., and his daughter Nina in the cast. In 1885, he produced his last good play, *The Jilt,* which opened in San Francisco on May 18. Shortly after, the Boucicault company sailed for Australia.

On September 9, 1885 an extraordinary event occurred when Boucicault was married in a registry office in Sydney to Louise

Thorndyke, a young actress in his company who had played opposite him in *The Jilt*. His brother Arthur, who had emigrated to Australia years before, witnessed the ceremony. In March, 1886, when the company had returned to New York to play *The Jilt*, Boucicault declared that he had never been legally married to Agnes. However, they had long been publicly recognized as man and wife, and Agnes was granted a divorce in England in the summer of 1888. After the formal announcement of the divorce on January 15, 1889, Boucicault went through another marriage ceremony with Louise Thorndyke. Not much is known of Louise, but apparently Dion was hopelessly infatuated with her. At least, that is what the portrait in *The Jilt* of Myles O'Hara's love for Kitty Woodstock would strongly suggest.

The Boucicault company continued to tour, and there were a few new plays. But Boucicault's luck had about run out and so had all of the money he had made on *The Shaughraun*. Finally, on April 30, 1888, the company was disbanded in Chicago; for the manager was out of funds. Still, he had a resource or two left; and he found a job with A. M. Palmer, who managed two New York theaters, as the head of a school of acting attached to the Madison Square Theatre. He also became a frequent contributor to *The North American Review*. By this time, the criticism of his last marriage had apparently died down; for on November 10, 1888, the Saturday Night Club of New York gave a banquet in his honor. Among the guests were Robert Ingersoll, General Sherman, Governor Flower, and Andrew Carnegie.

Boucicault still tried his hand at a play or two, but he was tiring, and early in 1890 he left Palmer's employ. He was working on an adaptation of Bret Harte's "The Luck of Roaring Camp" when he had a heart attack. He rallied from it, but then came down with pneumonia. On September 18, 1890, he died at his apartment at 103 West Fifty-fifth Street in New York. The funeral was on September 22 at the Church of the Transfiguration, "The Little Church around the Corner." His body was placed in a receiving vault at Woodlawn, and on December 19 he was buried in Mount Hope Cemetery.

Ibsen and Zola were writing now. The nineteenth-century theater was quickly passing away, and Boucicault passed away with it.

CHAPTER *2*

The Regency Comedies

BOUCICAULT'S first big success was *London Assurance* of 1841, and this play is really his only early one that is still remembered and occasionally anthologized. However, for a few years after 1841, until the pressure for ready money became irresistible, Boucicault was not totally a commercial dramatist who was willing to set his pen to any task or turn out any quick translation to order. For a few years, he retained the artistic standards he had held when writing *London Assurance*; and he did some good work.

Much of this early work has never been published, but there are at least three other published plays—the comedy *Old Heads and Young Hearts* and the farces *A Lover by Proxy* and *Alma Mater; or, A Cure for Coquettes*—that can rank with *London Assurance* as Boucicault's best. *London Assurance* was written because of Charles Mathews' request for a play about modern life. The play which Boucicault had originally submitted to Mathews was the one-act farce *A Lover by Proxy*. It, as well as the three-act farce *Alma Mater* and his best early comedy *Old Heads and Young Hearts*, was curiously enough not quite contemporary. Their settings seem to be the Regency period of 1811 to 1820; and, indeed, even *London Assurance*, although nominally set in the 1840's, has an earlier tone and flavor about it. I am rather at a loss to know why Boucicault chose this period rather than his own. Perhaps his early reading led him to it, or perhaps the first plays he saw, or perhaps this period of dashing bucks and gay blades spoke more directly to his own rattling exuberance. At any rate, this era of the *bon ton* is a relatively neglected one in the English drama; and Boucicault's pen brings it vividly back to life.

I   London Assurance

Edgar Allan Poe called *London Assurance* "that despicable mass in inanity." Dickens said, "The thing was as like any honest sympathy, or honest English, as the rose-pink on a sweep's face on May Day is to a beautiful complexion." Montrose J. Moses included it in an anthology "because it reflects the degradation of English comedy to the needs of a very trivial theatrical atmosphere." Indeed, Boucicault himself said that "It will not bear analysis as a literary production."

Despite that convincing array of opinion and despite the fact that the play's chief importance, historically and artistically, is theatrical, *London Assurance* still has a quite strong claim for consideration as literature. Admittedly, the piece is distinctly derivative; it imitates the manner of Sheridan and Goldsmith about three-quarters of a century after that manner had ceased even to pretend to hold the mirror up to nature. It has none of Sheridan's ability to create memorable situations and, therefore, great scenes. It has none of Goldsmith's warming geniality.

But *London Assurance* is probably, if literary influence has any significance at all, the most clear-cut bridge between the comedy of the late eighteenth century and the artificial comedy of Oscar Wilde in the 1890's. To a considerable extent, Wilde does seem a distinctly individual phenomenon, and such subsequent writers of artificial comedy as Somerset Maugham, Noel Coward, or P. G. Wodehouse probably also owe more to their individual views of contemporary society than they do to any deeply ingrained sense of theatrical tradition. For whatever it is worth, however, we can justly say that *London Assurance* was almost the only notable comedy of manners between the 1780's and the 1890's. If one is tracing growths and trends in the—to my mind—overzealous fashion of Allardyce Nicoll, the play has an indisputable importance for the history of English drama.

But it also has as much claim to literary merit as do most of the acceptable minor English comedies. It would certainly bear up well in comparison to the rather wooden comedy of Etherege, to the only fitfully excellent comedy of Steele, and to practically anything by writers like Colley Cibber, Aphra Behn, Hugh Kelly, or Richard Cumberland. Its position is rather like that of George

Lillo's *London Merchant*. Lillo's play stood almost alone in its time, being a significant forerunner of the play of bourgeois realism which slowly fermented all during the nineteenth century and then began to bubble over in the late 1890's with the coming of Jones, Pinero, Shaw, and the English productions of Ibsen. Boucicault's play stood almost in its time; but it did so as the last vital twitch of a dying manner, rather than as the first febrile twitch of a coming one. Its "despicable inanity" seems to me immensely more civilized than the puerile platitudes of the much-anthologized and respectable Lillo.

The plot of *London Assurance* is too traditional to detain us long. Its main action is concerned with the usual comic problem of whether boy gets girl, and onto this basic story are grafted various minor situations which illustrate the various foibles and follies of the minor characters. The main action is a love triangle between Sir Harcourt Courtly, his son young Courtly, and his fiancée Grace Harkaway. A proposed marriage between a young girl and an old rake is scarcely original, but originality of plot has never been a prime critical criterion for dramatic comedy.[1] This basic situation we find in Molière, in Jonson, in Shakespeare, and indeed as far back as Roman comedy; and the chief minor plot, about young sparks fleeing to the country to escape the city's dunning tradesmen, reminds us of Oliver Goldsmith's *She Stoops to Conquer* and George Farquhar's *The Beaux' Strategem*. The intrigue does not rise to any great scenes like the table-hiding scene in Molière's *Tartuffe* or the screen scene in Richard Brinsley Sheridan's *The School for Scandal*. But the intrigue has its traditional complications of misunderstandings and mistaken identity, and such masterpieces as Congreves' *The Way of the World* and Wilde's *The Importance of Being Earnest* have also survived quite well without great scenes.

Most of the characters are merely new versions of old stereotypes, such as the superannuated rake, the young lover, the clever servant, the intractable ingenue. However, Boucicault handles his stereotypes unusually well. Sir Harcourt Courtly is a caricature of a well-preserved old dandy, done with remarkable ease and urbanity. Dazzle, the friend of the nominal hero young Courtly, is a descendant of the comic servant, and an excellent one. Indeed, Charles Mathews, who produced the play originally with Madame

Vestris, took the role of Dazzle and made it a truly dazzling one. Pert, the heroine's maid, does not in the least wither in comparison with some of Molière's fine maids; and in his heroine, Grace Harkaway, Boucicault has created that delightful rarity, the intelligent heroine. To find her betters, we would have to go almost back to Millimant in Congreves' *The Way of the World* or forward to Vivie Warren in Bernard Shaw's *Mrs. Warren's Profession.*

Boucicault did have some failures of characterization in the play, notably in the figure of Mark Meddle, the stereotype of a lawyer. Meddle is a perfectly adequate theatrical character, an early day ambulance chaser who hopes to get someone to kick him or at least slander him so that he can go to court. The trouble with the character and with the jokes that arise from him is that Meddle is much more broadly drawn than the other roles. He is a mere theatrical grotesque; and the jokes about him, while good, are a bit too broad for art.

In two characters, Boucicault coined new stereotypes; and one of these characters, Lady Gay Spanker, is among the great acting parts of the century. She is a caricature of the horsey outdoorswoman, and her first appearance in the play was greeted with a delighted shock of recognition from the first-night audience. Mr. Spanker, her Milquetoast of a husband, is a good role although not nearly so showy; but his reversal from fuddled worm to momentarily belligerent lion is not the great scene that it should be.

Boucicault's dialogue is not quite memorable as literature, but it does have a fine theatrical ease. The dialogue in this play is closer to that of Vanbrugh than to that of Congreve, to that of Goldsmith than to that of Wilde. Boucicault has, like Wilde, his epigrams; but they lack the high polish and self-sufficiency of "I can resist everything except temptation" or "The youth of America is their oldest tradition. It has been going on now for three hundred years." A fairly typical Boucicaultian effort is an epigram such as, "Love ends in matrimony, wine in soda water." This works quite well in the context of the play on the stage, but it is hardly piquant enough to be included on its own merits in *Bartlett's Familiar Quotations.* The Wildean dialogue at its best is a thick rash of deftly turned witticisms hurrying one upon the other; the Boucicaultian dialogue more properly might be described as banter.

For example, in Act I, Max Harkaway invites the scapegrace Dazzle to Sir Harcourt's wedding under the mistaken impression that Dazzle is acquainted with Sir Harcourt:

MAX: . . . Sir, if you are not otherwise engaged, I shall feel honoured by your company at my house, Oak Hall, Gloucestershire.
DAZZLE: Your name is—
MAX: Harkaway—Max Harkaway.
DAZZLE: Harkaway—let me see—I ought to be related to the Harkaways somehow.
MAX: A wedding is about to come off—will you take a part on the occasion?
DAZZLE: With pleasure! Any part, but that of the husband.
MAX: Have you any previous engagement?
DAZZLE: I was thinking—eh! Why let me see. (*Aside*) Promised to meet my tailor and his account to-morrow; however, I'll postpone that. (*Aloud*) Have you good shooting?
MAX: Shooting! Why, there's no shooting at this time of the year.
DAZZLE: Oh! I'm in no hurry—I can wait till the season of course.

Much of the best dialogue in the play is humorous rather than witty, and it arises from the revelation of human foibles. In Sir Harcourt's first-act elucidation of the behavior of a gentleman, or in Lady Gay's third-act description of a hunt, we are more delighted by their quirks of character than by any great display of wit. A particularly fine example of this humorous revelation of foibles would be Dazzle's ingratiating fifth-act reply, when everyone finally turns on him and demands to know who he really is:

DAZZLE: Simple question as you may think it, it would puzzle half the world to answer. One thing I can vouch—Nature made me a gentleman—that is, I live on the best that can be procured for credit. I never spend my own money when I can oblige a friend. I'm always thick on the winning horse. I'm an epidemic on the trade of a tailor. For further particulars, inquire of any sitting magistrate.

This dialogue is not great; but, when spoken with the style which a Mathews could bring to it, it would seem almost brilliant in the theater. It is really no thinner than the dialogue of a Noel Coward or an S. N. Behrman, which, when spoken by the Lunts, takes on a similar sparkle in the theater.

It is scarcely an exaggeration to say that most dramatic dialogue in the nineteenth century was hopelessly bad. Its serious moments, even in the hands of the better writers such as Jerrold, Bulwer-Lytton, Charles Reade, or Tom Taylor was imitative, awkward, stilted, and artificial. The comic badinage was better; but, save for that of Planché in his best moments, it lacked suaveness, urbanity, and intelligence. Late in the century, Gilbert and Wilde wrote superbly in the comic vein; but even Wilde was impossibly artificial in his serious moments. Indeed, some of the worst dialogue ever written by a great dramatist occurs in the serious moments of Oscar Wilde's plays.

Possibly the reason for this poor quality lies in the fact that there was no longer an established literary mode for the dramatist. The drama had largely degenerated into melodrama, spectacle, and low buffoonery. For a literary model, a dramatist was really thrown back to the eighteenth century; and this Boucicault play does look back to eighteenth-century comedy. It was a remarkable play for a dramatist barely twenty years old to have written; and, in the context of its time, its excellence is notable. But Boucicault could hardly hope singlehandedly to turn back the clock. The English drama was drifting slowly toward a realistic, serious portrayal of life; and a comedy of manners like *London Assurance*, fine though it was, could hardly stem that slow but inexorable tide.

If it is possible to consider the play out of the context of its time in order to determine its residue of artistry, I think we must judge that *London Assurance* is far from the contemptible inanity that Poe judged it. It is a highly competent, highly playable comedy of manners, and on its own merits it may take a respectable position among the minor dramas of the English stage. Had Boucicault been born in the eighteenth century when the comedy of manners was still a usable dramatic mode, he might have gone from strength to strength.

II *Two Farces*

Although the one-act farce *A Lover by Proxy* was rejected by Mathews, it was subsequently performed on April 21, 1842, at the Haymarket. For awhile it achieved some popularity as an after-piece, but it was a one-act farce and almost certain, therefore, to fall into an ultimate obscurity. Still, it is a consummately charm-

ing farce. Its characters are finely drawn for this broad genre;
and the elegant, rattling, half-addlepated young blood of a hero,
Harry Lawless, is a theatrical creation of a high order. The dialogue is remarkably polished for a farce and is full of rapid-fire
badinage and theatrical quips. Indeed, even at its flattest, it has a
saving drollery. The following inconsequential bit from the beginning of the play has a fine Jeeves-Bertie Wooster ring to it:

BLUSHINGTON (*Putting his head out of his bed-room door, in flat C.
    with his nightcap on*): Nibbs!
NIBBS: Sir.
BLUSHINGTON: Some soda water.
NIBBS: 'Tis on your dressing table, sir.
BLUSHINGTON: Nibbs, who has been at my razors?
NIBBS: Mr. Lawless, he cut open the champagne corks with them last
    night.
BLUSHINGTON: Nibbs?
NIBBS: Sir.
BLUSHINGTON: Nothing.
NIBBS: Very well, sir.

A more usual passage is the following one whose concluding
speech is enlivened with a still effective theatrical fancy:

LAWLESS: Peter, my boy, how are you, will you do me a favour?
BLUSHINGTON: Certainly. . . .
LAWLESS: Just let me kick that chap of ours out of the window.
    . . . Oh! he's off—lucky for him—you spoil him, Peter.
BLUSHINGTON: But if he would not go faster—
LAWLESS: Let me have him for a week; I'd give him a new motive
    power—the rascal looks as if he lived on cane-bottom chairs and
    soporifics. Observe, Squib, there's a picture—what a face—like a
    second hand anvil, you might peg away at it for half an hour and
    only split your knuckles—small eye—black habit—long chin—
    sharp nature! Mouth, minus two teeth—(*spars*)—fancy! Legs, a
    pair of parenthesis—no infernal ramrod stuck in a brick. Then,
    his body balanced on the top like a stick of sealing wax on a care-
    fully selected merry-thought.

Despite the purposeful inconsequence of much of the dialogue,
the plot gallops along at a spanking pace; and the piece has lost
little vigor in the last hundred years. Eminently playable still, it

deserves to be back in print. It is as adequate as literature, as, say, Garrick's excellent short farce *The Lying Valet*, and it is considerably better written than more famous farces like *Charley's Aunt* or *Abie's Irish Rose*.

A Cure for Coquettes; or, Alma Mater is a three-act farce produced on September 19, 1842, at the Haymarket. Despite its Oxford setting and some local-color jokes about undergraduate life, the play is basically a conventional one about what boy will get what girl. Its plot seems in the reading at least a bit too complicated because of the large cast. Still, the characters are well-drawn and successful—particularly Sir Samuel Sarcasm, the elderly lover whose cutting tongue alienates people; "Count" Pave, the humorless society adventurer; Gradus, Sir Samuel's bookworm nephew whose timidity makes him stutter inordinately; and Pliant, the student who agrees with everyone.

There are also some farcically superb situations. Especially notable is the closing of Act II when Tom Venture, the hero, is discovered holding a forbidden party with his friends in his rooms at college. They attempt to explain away the remains of the feast, which is now scattered over the floor, by asserting that the dishes and lobsters are so disposed in order to represent troop movements at the battle of Thermopylae. Unfortunately, the incongruously drunken Gradus then breaks out of the closet, in which he has been secreted, blowing a trombone.

The dialogue is the same breezy, witty banter of which Boucicault was a master, and there is a good deal of farcically adroit stage business—as when two men, approaching Sir Samuel from opposite directions to shake his hand, wind up shaking each other's. The piece certainly belongs to a minor genre, but it is, like *A Lover by Proxy*, thoroughly successful in what it attempts. Indeed, it would seem nearly as droll today as it did in 1842.

III   Old Heads and Young Hearts

Old Heads and Young Hearts, a nearly forgotten but thoroughly admirable play, was first acted on November 18, 1844, at the Haymarket, London, with Mathews as "Littleton Coke" and Madame Vestris as "Lady Alice." In plot, characterization, and dialogue, it ranks among the finest comic efforts of the nineteenth-century English stage; and to my mind it is even a considerable improvement upon Boucicault's first success, *London Assurance*.

It is largely a tale of Regency high life with an ingeniously tangled plot involving two interlocking love triangles. The beauty of the plot is its large number of absurd situations which arise from Boucicault's deft use of misunderstandings, talking at cross purposes, mistaken identity, and disguise. When the piece is played at a good, fast pace, the fertile invention of the author, in devising ever more absurd complications, should be seen to excellent advantage.

Two of the most delightful situations might have sprung straight from Restoration comedy. Littleton Coke and Lady Anne, like the Restoration beau and belle, are both intent on disguising their own emotions and in surprising the other into the first admission of love. First, Coke carries on a conversation with Lady Anne, while urbanely writing a love letter; and her reactions are a droll mélange of hope that it may be for her and exasperation that it might not. Later, she turns the tables on him:

LITTLETON: . . . She takes a letter from her breast—'tis to me. (*She opens it*) No—she opens it—she reads it—(*She sighs*) she is affected—what can it mean?

LADY ANNE: Mr. Coke—I—hurt my hand this evening and am unable to write—would you have the kindness to answer, for me, this letter, and write as I tell you?

LITTLETON: Write as!—(*Aside*) What does she—perhaps 'tis from Tom—it is—I—

LADY ANNE (*Having settled the writing materials for him*): Pray be seated. (*He sits*) Now, will you promise me to write as I tell you?

LITTLETON (*Aside*): She smiles, ah!—(*Aloud*) I'll swear it.

LADY ANNE: "My dear"—let's see—yes—"dear sir"—

LITTLETON: Two adjectives?

LADY ANNE: Ye-s! "If (*reading letter*) fondest hopes"—poor fellow!—"if you imagine my treatment of you to be cruel"—

LITTLETON (*Aside*): Damme, if she isn't making me write a love letter to somebody; oh, that's too good! (*Rises and throws down pen*)

LADY ANNE: Bad pen? Don't stir, here's another. . . .

The characterization of the play is mainly that of hard comedy with two intrusions of sentiment. The straight characters of the four lovers are basically the Restoration beau and belle, although both Coke and Lady Anne are a bit more developed. Coke is a rather good proud scapegrace, while Lady Anne is built along the lines of the dashing urban hoyden, à la Georgette Heyer's "The Grand Sophy." The minor characters are effective "humors": Lord Pompion, a fine and crotchety old Tory; his wife who is genteelly addicted to the brandy bottle; Colonel Rockett, a neat cartoon of the explosive, retired military man with a soft heart and a hard vocabulary; and Bob, a comic servant who might easily stand up with Garrick's lying valet.

Bob, incidentally, has one brilliantly conceived scene. In the disguise of a solicitor, he is being interviewed by Lord Pompion who inquires about an illegitimate son he had years earlier entrusted to Bob's supposed firm. Bob, remembering an old trick that Lord Pompion's legitimate son Charles had played on him, decides to pay Charles back in kind. Charles has just shaved off his whiskers in order to pose as Miss Rockett's coachman, and to his irritation and discomfiture Bob introduces him to his father as the presumptive bastard.

The two sentimental intrusions in the play are a good deal more effective than those of much eighteenth-century sentimental comedy. The most notable is Jesse Rural, the elderly minister who had been Littleton Coke's tutor. The old man is totally baffled by the complications of the action; and he compounds, in his well-meaning fashion, the confusion in the worst way. However, our laughter at him is extremely good-natured, for Boucicault draws him as the most kindhearted old man in the world. Certainly, a poorer writer would have played up the absurdity of the old man or the pathos; but Boucicault successfully threads his way between Dickensian bathos and Jonsonian flintheartedness. The ensuing result is rather rare for the drama.

The other soft character is Coke's older brother, Tom. For Littleton's good, Tom has refused to countenance his extravagances, and the two brothers have become estranged. Further, Tom has the misfortune to fall in love with Lady Anne, the object of Littleton's affections. The scene in which Tom loses the girl is played with such a diffident restraint, however, that one would have to call its basic tone realistic rather than sentimental.

The dialogue of the play is generally of high quality. Its usual tone is a cut above the easy banter of *London Assurance*, and one symptom of the fact is its use of many more of the devices of wit —such as wordplay, parallelisms, metaphor, and image. Yet, despite this greater fullness of rhetorical devices, Boucicault

manages to avoid the artificiality of an Oscar Wilde. His dialogue
has, even today, a conversational ease about it. One method of
attaining this ease is a crafty use of the sentence fragment, as
may be seen in the dialogue quoted between Coke and Lady
Anne. Or, to illustrate how smoothly the wit is introduced into
the flow of dialogue, we should note the general fluency of this
following minor exchange, and how easily Lady Pompion's fine
concluding remark rises out of it:

ROEBUCK: My dearest mother!
LADY POMPION: Ah! Charles, how d'ye do, dear? (*Lifts her eye-glass*)
     Bless me, how brown you're grown—for heaven's sake, take care
     of Bichon, there. (*Shakes his hand over the dog*) Have you
     brought me the Eau de Cologne?
ROEBUCK: Yes, everything—but, my dear mother—
LADY POMPION: Dear—how old he looks for a son of mine.

In recent years, *Old Heads and Young Hearts* has been anthologized only once, and that fact is a great pity; for, even more than
London Assurance, it is a play for the living stage. As literature, it
is bettered only by Oscar Wilde in its own century; and it may
easily be ranked beside the best minor drama of the eighteenth
century.

CHAPTER 3

The Commercial Potboilers

IT is probably somewhat arbitrary to categorize Boucicault's commercial plays, for the categories tend to blend into each other. Still, an attempt may help us understand the main characteristics of the bulk of Boucicault's work. We might, then, consider his commercial plays as falling into these basic types: the straight translation, in which Boucicault added little or nothing of his own; the adaptation, in which he added something of his own work—and sometimes that something bulked very large; the spectacular melodrama; and the pseudo work of art.

I *The Translations*

Although Boucicault did not always credit the original authors with a by-line, he produced and published a good many straightforward translations. He was fluent in French and was abreast of what was happening on the Paris stage. So, whenever he needed a new piece and had nothing original ready to hand, it was, as he once remarked, "child's play" to dash off a translation. He brought to this work his own facility in shaping dialogue, and sometimes he succeeded in making what sounded stiff and mannered in the original seem easier in translation. Ultimately, however, the theatrical excellence or poverty of these translations is due mainly to their original authors.

Pauvrette, for instance, of 1858, is a trivial romantic entertainment, based on the hoary old contrivance of children switched in the cradle. Some of its sentiment was put in by Boucicault, but mainly its threadbare theatrical thrills and tears were in the original script by Desnoyer and Dennery. *Jezebel; or, The Dead Reckoning* of 1870 is a creaky romantic drama that never rises above the original tired devices of Anicet-Bourgeois and Michel Masson in their *Le Pendu.*

Some of Boucicault's translations were of better plays and were quite successful and profitable when transplanted. *Sixtus V; or, The Broken Vow*, or as it was later called *The Pope of Rome*, is a translation written with John Bridgeman of *L'Abbaye de Castro* by Dinaux and Lemoine. It is a quite effective play of melo-dramatic intrigue and allowed Dion a fine swashbuckling role as Hugo, the middle-aged soldier of fortune. Still, most of the the-atrical excellence of the play was in the original version.

The same can be said of *The Corsican Brothers; or, The Ven-detta.* This popular piece is an adaptation of *Les Frères Corses* by Grangé and Montépin, which was in turn based on a story by Dumas. It is beautiful melodramatic theater, and Charles Kean played to the hilt the dual role of the twins. Years later Henry Irving found that the old play had lost little of its effect; indeed, in our own time the story has been made into a rattling good adventure film with Douglas Fairbanks, Jr. Boucicault brought little to the work, but he did not really need to.

He also brought little to *Louis XI*, his translation from Casimir Delavigne. Although the play has no standing as literature, the decrepit old king offered a fine theatrical challenge, and both Kean and Irving kept the play in their repertoires.

This list might be considerably extended, but the only point to be made from Boucicault's prolific translating is that, at worst, he did this journeyman work quite adequately.

II *The Adaptations*

In a sense, we could call perhaps 90 per cent of Boucicault's work adaptation, for most of his plays borrow in one way or an-other from earlier writers. His revisions of Colman's *John Bull* and of Otway's *Venice Preserved* apparently stay fairly close to the originals. So also do many of his French plays. *Led Astray*, for instance, is almost a straight translation of Feuillet's *La Tenta-tion*, but to this pre-Ibsen domestic drama about the double stand-ard Boucicault did add the minor role of the society card-sharper Major O'Hara. It would seem, however, that even when Bouci-cault did little, the little that he did was significant. As Frank Dalton remarks:

> There is no denying his audacity. What could be more daring than when at the Old Royal he presented a new comedy called

"Dennis O'Dowd," which proved to be George Coleman's [*sic*] popular comedy, "John Bull"? It was a shock to us all. Old Davy Byng, in particular, simply fumed, "D——d insolence! outrageous presumption! cheek! fraud!"

We played it, and then wondered. The comedy distinctly improved. Dennis Brulgruddery's "shebeen" became the village hotel, with the genial Dennis O'Dowd as the prosperous and no less humorous landlord. This, with many slight alterations, changing of absurd names, revising old jokes about stale beer, etc., altered the play so materially as to raise it from the level of character farce to the exalted region of high comedy. Rightly, or wrongly, the object was accomplished, audaciously, of course, but at the price of rather small change.[1]

In *Kerry; or, Night and Morning*, adapted from Emile de Girardin's *La Joie Fait Peur*, Boucicault kept the basic structure of the original, but built up the part of the old servant, changing him into an Irishman and making him the main character as well as a fat acting part for himself. *Andy Blake; or, The Irish Diamond*, adapted from Alfred Bayard's *Le Gamin de Paris*, is even more thoroughly worked over. Not only is Andy's character thoroughly Dionized, but the whole tone of the play has been drastically changed by setting the action in Dublin.

Some of Boucicault's most drastic deviations from his original models were his dramatizations of short stories and novels. Sometimes he improved upon the original; at other times he came notably acropper. At any rate, a consideration of a few such successes and failures might suggest some tentative generalizations about adapting fiction for the stage.

The adaptation of *Foul Play*, for example, is really a foul play. The original is now a little-read novel which Boucicault wrote with Charles Reade, the eminent Victorian man of letters. Although the characters through much of the book remain stiffly stereotypical, *Foul Play* is still a surprisingly engrossing entertainment. The attraction lies less in the complicated plot—part of which Boucicault seems to have borrowed from *Le Portefeuille Rouge* by Narcisse Fournier and Henri-Horace Meyer—but in the situation that takes up the book's long middle section.

The hero, a wrongly accused ticket-of-leave man, and the heroine are on a ship which is scuttled by the captain and the first mate. The story of their survival in a long boat, of the death of their companions, and of their ultimate discovery of a desert island is the good, sound stuff of the adventure yarn. But, once on the island, the story becomes more than merely sound. The castaway situtation, of course, à la Robinson Crusoe, is an always intriguing one; but Reade and Boucicault made some attractive improvements on Defoe. The main charm of this section is that the hero changes from a traditional stereotype into a sort of Shavian version of the Admirable Crichton. He is a walking encyclopedia of knowledge about navigation, botany, carpentry, pottery, agriculture, anthropology, marine life, history, and literature; and his ingenuity dwarfs poor Crusoe's. This section is hardly photographic realism, but it is realistic enough for an adventure yarn, and it is also thoroughly delightful.

In the book's last section, the heroine is delivered while the hero remains on the island, and she returns to England to clear his name. We have here something of the charm of the detective story with, to my mind, none of the irritation of the hyperintricate puzzle. We know the culprit, but the heroine does not. Also, the heroine is not so cunning as the culprit, and so she is constantly balked. Much of the pleasure, then, comes from no super-Sherlockian ratiocination but from the way in which she draws sympathetic people to aid her and from some curious lore about the detection of forged handwriting.

This description is of the kind of book that is rather far removed from the realm of art. Still, it is good entertainment, despite its Victorian trappings; and it does make many contemporary tales of intrigue—particularly those rain-drenched and dreary stories of Graham Greene and John Le Carre—appear as joyless as they actually are. It is probably impossible to unravel who wrote what with any exactitude, but my reading of Reade suggests that the superb middle section is mainly his, while the more conventional characters and the intricate plotting of the beginning and end are Boucicault's. The book is hardly fine enough to rank with Robert Louis Stevenson's *Treasure Island,* John Buchan's *John MacNab,* or J. R. R. Tolkien's *The Hobbit;* but it is beguiling enough for the bedside reader to turn to from time to time with pleasant expectations.

Boucicault and Reade fell out about the dramatization of the novel, and both made attempts at it. Boucicault's is a rather instructive attempt, for the necessities of the drama forced him to compress. The result is that the poorer parts of the novel remain in the play while the better parts are absent. All of the exciting twists of the plot remain, but there is little of the original engaging humor. Also, the plot in the play is so stressed that the characterization is much flatter than that of the novel. The hero of the play is now only a long-suffering stock character full of platitudes and nobility, but the once attractive heroine is now only another faceless ingenue of the nineteenth-century drama.

In considering Boucicault's adaptations from novels, we are tempted to generalize that he seemed to improve on poor work and to make good work worse. This is probably an inevitable situation, for most novels are too complex for the stage to do more than suggest their basic quality. Many of the nineteenth-century dramatizations of Scott and Dickens left in only the excitements of the plot and left out every literary excellence that gave the originals body and substance; and this would seem to be the case certainly in Boucicault's *Smike*, which dramatizes Dickens' *Nicholas Nickleby;* his *Jeanie Deans,* which dramatizes Scott's *The Heart of Mid-Lothian;* or his *Clarissa Harlowe,* which attempts the impossible task of dramatizing Richardson's novel. Really, it was, as we shall see, only in *The Colleen Bawn,* Boucicault's adaptation of Gerald Griffin's *The Collegians,* that he made a thorough success of dramatizing a novel. But the reason in this case seemed to be that he made no great attempt to be faithful to the original. He took the situation from Griffin and left everything else, refashioning, adding, and twisting the original characters, with his eye not upon the page but the stage.

A long work of fiction is much less adaptable to the stage than a short one. This point seems borne out by Boucicault's very successful dramatizations of *The Cricket on the Hearth* and *Rip Van Winkle.* No one but a totally confirmed devotee of Dickens could find much to admire in *The Cricket on the Hearth.* This short Christmas story is basically a blend of trite melodrama and perfunctory infusions of broadly grotesque comedy. The comedy sometimes seems so baldly done as to be almost a parody of the Dickens manner, and the whole is smothered in a sentimentality which is both cloying and conventional. The conventionally melodramatic, sentimental, and comic, however, never appear quite so bald on the stage as they do on the page. And, while Boucicault's 1859 adaptation of the story, *Dot,* is worth little more literary consideration than Dickens' story, it was effective theater. Indeed, as entertainment, it might still prove an attractive offering for the Christmas season. It offers several meaty roles, some songs, some dances, some opportunity for spectacle; and its pathos is nicely balanced by its comedy.

The character of Tilly Slowboy, for instance, is little more than a typical Dickens grotesque on the page. When dramatized, as in the following scene, it offers fine theatrical comic possibilities:

DOT: Here, help to set the table. John will be home ere his supper's ready. Put the kettle on the fire, while I lay the tea. Handy now, handy!

TILLY: Ees, mums. (*Goes to fire for kettle, shifts the baby from one arm to the other awkwardly. Takes kettle*)

DOT: Then toast the bacon, Tilly. Come, quick, lass.

TILLY: Ees, mums! (*Runs to flitch of bacon L., gets bewildered between bacon, kettle, and baby*)

DOT: Why put the child to bed, you goose, and the kettle on the fire.

TILLY: Oh, ees, mums. (*Runs down. Puts kettle in cradle L. and is going with child to fire*)

DOT: Oh! My gracious, Tilly! (*Snatches child*) You horrid thing! She was going to boil the child.

TILLY: No, mums. (*Goes to cradle L. and rocks it*)

DOT: And now she be a-rocking the kettle. The lass be crazy sure. (*Takes kettle out*)

TILLY: Ow! Ow! Ow! (*Cries*) Oh, mums, please don't scold. I couldn't help it. Ow! Ow!

It would be almost impossible to make this scene in a work of fiction seem anything other than idiotic; but, with its basic laughter arising from two visual shocks to the audience, it is very canny theater. And, indeed, the quality of this scene is generally the quality of the whole play.

Boucicault also diverges from Dickens by including a rhymed prologue which is a fairy vision and which offers some opportunity for spectacle and stresses what theme the play has. He rearranges the plot slightly so that the identity of the Deaf Old Man is known almost immediately to the audience, and there is no possibility of confusion about Dot's character. Doubtless, Boucicault loses some suspense in this way, but that is better than losing one's audience.

In typical fashion, Boucicault also introduces a technical novelty in an early use of the wagon stage, in order to arouse delight and wonder by a visual device. The scene was described in the London *Times:*

> The situation by which this jealousy [John Peerybingle's of Ned Plummer] is aroused is also contrived in a manner entirely novel. To show the part of the action that takes place in Caleb Plummer's room, his cottage is regularly built upon the stage, a wall being left open to show the interior, while the rest of the picture is filled with the farmyard and stable, covered with snow. When Tackleton would call the attention of John Peerybingle to the conduct of Dot with the stranger, the cottage, with all the personages in it, gradually slides to the side of the stage, leaving the courtyard in the middle, with John in frantic despair at the scene he witnessed in the building on the opposite side.[2]

One of the most enduringly popular of nineteenth-century plays was *Rip Van Winkle,* in the version used by the famous American actor Joseph Jefferson. It is impossible to tell just how large a hand Boucicault had in this version, but I am inclined to think it was a quite large one. There had been several previous dramatizations of Washington Irving's story, and Jefferson himself had already acted in one unsuccessful version. In 1865, Jefferson, who had acted in New York with Boucicault in *Dot* and in *The Octoroon,* was in London and wanted a strong piece for his debut. Boucicault took the version that Jefferson had already acted, and the result was a resounding success which became Jefferson's most famous role.

This version differs from the previous ones in many significant ways—in the structure and incidents of its plot, in having fewer and more fully drawn characters, and in the dialogue almost throughout. "How much of this difference," remarks Arthur Hobson Quinn, "is due to Boucicault it is of course now impossible to say, but since Mr. Jefferson undoubtedly made changes from time to time it is safe to assume that by the time the play was printed in 1895 it was mostly his own."[3] Townsend Walsh remarks, "That the success of Boucicault's version of 'Rip' was due almost solely to Jefferson's acting, I do most potently believe. That Washington Irving's scant little story was an unactable proposition till Boucicault touched it with his wizard's wand, is proven by history."[4] But, despite its great success, Walsh's final judgment is that the play is "the veriest potboiler." With this view, Boucicault himself agreed:

> . . . I took down Washington Irving's story and read it over. It was hopelessly undramatic. "Joe," I said, "this old sot is not a pleasant figure. He lacks romance. I dare say you made a fine sketch of the old beast, but there is no interest in him. He may be picturesque, but he is not dramatic. I would prefer to start him in a play as a young scamp—thoughtless, gay, just such a curly-headed, good-humored fellow as all the village girls would love, and the children and dogs would run after.
>
> Jefferson threw up his hands in despair. It was totally opposed to his artistic preconception. But I insisted, and he reluctantly conceded.
>
> Well, I wrote the play as he plays it now. It was not much of a literary production, and it was with some apology that it was handed to him. He read it, and when he met me I said: "It's a poor thing, Joe." "Well," he replied, "it is good enough for me." It was produced. Three or four weeks afterward he called on me, and his first words were "You were right about making *Rip* [*sic*] a young man. Now I could not conceive and play him in any other shape." [5]

Despite both Walsh's and Boucicault's disclaimers, *Rip Van Winkle* is an excellent play; and Boucicault's notion that he should "sweep aside Washington Irving, and make Rip a young buoyant ne'er-do-well . . ." resulted in a fascinating character study. Some contemporary critics compared this new Rip with Boucicault's own Irish heroes, but there is a considerable difference. Myles na Coppaleen, Shaun the Post, and Conn the Shaughraun are all basically goodhearted, sunny characters; their flaws are ones that stem from exuberance of spirit. Rip has some of the same qualities—an innate canniness, a warm joviality, and a Falstaffian slipperiness and gift for banter. But he has also a few untheatrical, unsympathetic, and ineradicable flaws of character. The two most notable are his very real dislike of his carping wife and his drunkenness. In the early part of the play, Rip's view of the nagging Gretchen is quite untouched by any qualifying theatrical affection. This situation is interestingly close to reality and quite far from the simplified verities of the stage and of Boucicault's own usual theatrical practice. Also, Rip's drinking is considerably more ingrained and serious than that of Myles na

Coppaleen or Conn the Shaughraun, Boucicault's own Irish scamps. Myles and Conn drink with spirit and gusto, and the effect is merely an intensification of their own high spirits. Neither needs drink, but Rip is addicted to it; and once again we are much closer to the world of reality than to the world behind the footlights.

With these unsympathetic and honestly drawn flaws, Boucicault's Rip is a full, rich, and complex character who is inestimably better than the previous theatrical Rips or, indeed, than Irving's own. Also, it is rather a *tour de force* for a dramatist to succeed in making basically sympathetic a character so distant from the usual naïve stereotypes of the drama. It is no exaggeration to consider Boucicault's Rip as one of the great character roles of nineteenth-century theater.

No one familiar with the quality of Boucicault's dialogue could mistake his particular touch in this play. The easy flow of quips that reveal character is one of the major charms and excellences of the play. To take one example, the second-act dialogue between Rip and Gretchen could, with a change from Dutch accent to Irish brogue, almost be given to Conn the Shaughraun and his nagging mother. The business, incidentally, at the window in this scene, when Rip does not at first see Gretchen inside, is reminiscent of that at the window in the second scene of *Arrah-na-Pogue*. And, the following typical dialogue is interestingly close to the letter dialogue quoted from *The Shaughraun* in the next chapter. Rip wants to know what is in the paper but, like Conn, wants also to disguise the fact of his own illiteracy:

RIP: What do you learn mit that school,—pretty much something? (*Laughing at his mistake*) I mean, everything?
HENDRICK: Yes; reading, writing and arithmetic.
RIP: Reading, and what?
HENDRICK: And writing, and arithmetic.
RIP (*Puzzled*): Writing and what?
HENDRICK: Arithmetic.
RIP (*More puzzled*): What meticks is that?
HENDRICK: Arithmetic.
RIP (*With profound astonishment and patting Hendrick's head*): I don't see how the little mind can stand it all. Can you read?
HENDRICK: Oh, yes!
RIP (*With a serious affectation of incredulity*): I don't believe it; now,

I'm just goin' to see if you can read. If you can't read, I won't let
you marry my daughter. No, sir. (*Very drolly*) I won't have nobody in my family what can't read. (*Taking out the paper that
Derrick has given him*) Can you read ritmatics like that?

HENDRICK: Yes, that's writing.

RIP (*Nonplussed*): Oh! I thought it was reading.

HENDRICK: It's reading and writing, too.

RIP: What, both together. (*Suspiciously looking at the paper*) Oh,
yes; I didn't see that before; go long with it.

Act III of the play, in the Catskills when Rip meets Henry Hud-
son and his crew, has some opportunities for spectacular staging
which Boucicault, with his penchant for the vividly visual, must
have included. It is a night scene with a furious rainstorm. There
is a swollen stream spilling down the mountainside and later,
when the sky clears, an impressive vista of the country below.

With all of these qualities—an engrossing story, one superbly
full character, much still fluent and amusing dialogue, and one
scene calling for spectacular staging—it is not surprising that the
play was the success of Jefferson's career. Indeed, the play does
not seem to warrant Boucicault's and Walsh's strictures. It seems
to me to rank easily among Boucicault's best and freest adaptations, and I should think that its entertainment value is still little
dissipated by the passage of a hundred years.

Using Boucicault's adaptations as cases in point, perhaps the
ultimate generalization that can be made is that the dramatist is
most successful when he uses his original as an inspiration rather
than as a model.

III   *The Spectacular Melodramas*

Perhaps the best way to begin a discussion of Boucicault's potboiling entertainments is to glance at a very successful one which
contains most of the form's typical ingredients. *The Poor of New
York, The Streets of New York, The Poor of Liverpool, The Streets
of London, The Streets of Dublin, The Streets of Philadelphia,*
and *The Money Panic of '57* are all the same play. An adaptation
of *Les Pauvres de Paris* by Brisebarre and Nus, Boucicault originally performed the piece at Wallack's Theatre in New York on
December 8, 1857, under the title of *The Poor of New York*. A

few years later in Liverpool, Boucicault resurrected the piece; thereafter he merely changed the title and the locale according to wherever he played it. It was extremely successful, and Samuel French's, amazingly enough, still has it in print. Dickens, however, remarked about it: "It is the most depressing instance, without exception, of an utterly degrading and debasing theatrical taste that has ever come under my notice. For not only do the audiences—of all classes—go, but they are unquestionably delighted." [5] Commenting upon it and similar efforts, Boucicault himself observed, "I can spin out these rough-and-tumble dramas as a hen lays eggs. It's a degrading occupation, but more money has been made out of guano than out of poetry." [6] That line, incidentally, might almost be taken as his epitaph.

The Poor of New York may truly stand as typical of the popular potboilers which Boucicault turned out in great number. As literature, it is hopeless drivel and far below Boucicault's ability. He is in this play purely an entertainment pander, and he includes every traditionally effective theatrical device that he can work in. He has a complicated plot concerning a lost fortune and lovers who are parted by cruel circumstance. He adds a dash of broadly Dickensian humor. He provides a soupçon of real observation. He includes the difficult and exciting spectacular scene of a burning tenement. He allots a just distribution of rewards and punishments. Indeed, every stale staple of the popular theater seems to turn up in *The Poor of New York*—virtue in distress, noble magnanimity, sinister unscrupulousness, a rousing fight, a scrap of paper which will make all come right, a feast, a wedding, the moderate but not original novelty of a dual action on a divided stage, and an appropriately platitudinous moral that is cannily calculated to offend no segment of any audience anywhere. Everything is theatrical rather than real, traditional rather than individual, hackneyed rather than original. His evil financier, Gideon Bloodgood, grinds the faces of the poor, and the poor themselves are long-suffering, selfless, clean, honest, hopeful, thrifty, and Godfearing. The emotions suffered are invariably phrased in the most conventional stock terms.

Here, for instance, is the old sea captain, who will soon be cheated of his money and die of apoplexy. He is speaking to Bloodgood about his family:

. . . tears of joy come into my eyes whenever I think of those children—and my dear wife, the patient, devoted companion of the old
sailor, whose loving voice murmurs each evening a prayer for those
who are on the sea; and my children, sir, two little angels; one a
fair little thing—we call her Lucy—she is my youngest—all red
and white like a little bundle of flowers; and my eldest—my son,
Paul—we named him after Paul Jones—a sailor's whim; well, sir,
when the ship is creaking and groaning under my feet, when the
squall drives the hail and sleet across my face, amidst the thunder,
I only hear three voices—through the gloom I can see only three
faces pressed together like three angels waiting for me in heaven,
and that heaven is my home. . . .

One symptom, I think, of the theater's improvement in the last
hundred years is that a Laurence Olivier would have trouble now
with that speech. Really, this passage approaches the nadir of
Boucicault, and yet the piece was immensely popular and made
a great deal of money. It made money because it thrilled people,
it held them on the edges of their seats with excitement, it drew
forth gales of laughter, and it evoked buckets of tears. Appallingly
banal as it is, it was at one time good theater; and it is so cannily
constructed that, with a little bit of rewriting of the most maudlin
parts, it might even still work. That point seems to imply that the
theater is an almost idiotically naïve art in the hands of all but its
greatest practitioners. That implication is probably still quite true.
Writing a play is still rather like trying to paint a masterpiece
with the talent of a Chester Gould or a Chic Young.

From *The Poor of New York*, we can see that even Boucicault's
spectacular melodramas were not quite of a piece. Despite their
simple emotionalism and platitudinous statement, they were a
blend of farce, pathos, and fast-paced action. Their most striking
feature, however, was the "sensation scene" which has been per-
ceptively discussed by George Rowell:

None of his melodramas would be complete without a thrilling se-
quence on which the resources of the Victorian theatre were fully
extended to produce a novel and spectacular effect. The attempted
drowning in *The Colleen Bawn;* the exploding steamboat in *The
Octoroon;* the house burnt down in *The Poor of New York;*
Shaun's ascent of the prison tower in *Arrah-na-Pogue;* the boat-
race rowed in *Formosa*—all were triumphs of ingenuity, accu-
rately aimed at their audience's level. Moreover a detailed in-

vestigation has recently disclosed how Boucicault's innovations foreshadow such fundamentals of film-making as cross-cutting, tracking, and panning.[7] In short, the sensation scenes of Boucicault's plays are not merely more ingenious than those of a Moncreiff or Fitzball. They are expertly woven into the fabric of the play, so that they emerge as the pivot of the story, not its *raison d'être;* nor is the novelty of the sensation scene made the excuse for a total lack of character, plausibility, or intelligence. Boucicault was above all things thorough.[8]

None of the melodramas is worth extended discussion or worth taking seriously. If, however, one is able to take them frivolously, in the way that one views a modern adventure film or a television "Western," then the following plays would probably be the ones most worth mentioning.

The Vampire (or *The Phantom* as it was called in its later shortened version) is a delightful bit of spooky *Kitsch* about the vampire of Raby Castle in Wales, who keeps appearing over the centuries and who uses the excellently sinister *nom de guerre* of Gervase Rookwood. This 1852 melodrama counterpoints a good deal of effective theatrical humor in the low characters against the pasteboard horrors of the main plot.

The year 1858 saw two very successful Boucicault melodramas. The first was *Jessie Brown; or, The Relief of Lucknow.* Like the previous year's *The Poor of New York,* the play was based on a quite contemporary event, the siege of the Lucknow garrison in September, 1857. The play is full of shooting, fighting, heroics, and patriotism; and several of its incidents have frequently been reused in such films as *Gunga Din* and *The Charge of the Light Brigade.* The same year's *Pauvrette* is a bit of romantic folderol whose action is initiated by the not particularly fresh notion of two babies being mistakenly switched in the cradle. Its most notable scene is the spectacular avalanche in the Alps in Act III: "Rocks and precipices occupy the stage. A rude hut on one side, in front. A bridge formed by a felled tree crosses the chasm, at the back."

The avalanche itself must have been forbiddingly difficult to stage, for "Large blocks of hardened snow and masses of rock fall, rolling into the abyss . . . the bridge is broken and hurled into the abyss—the paths have been filled with snow and now an immense sheet rushing down from the [Right] entirely buries the whole scene to the height of twelve or fifteen feet swallowing up the cabin and leaving above a clear level sea of snow." The hero and heroine are buried in this cabin for several months until the spring thaw, but Boucicault neglects to mention how they managed to breathe.

The year 1866 was a prolific year for Boucicault, and he later described the inception of three of this year's plays:

> At a dinner party which took place in 1866, the question was discussed as to the value of the literary merit of a play that had recently been produced. One side maintained that the literary element in a drama was rather an impediment than an assistance to popular success.
>
> "Gentlemen," said the host, "Will you permit that this question be settled practically? I propose to write three new pieces; one a society drama, relying mainly on its literary treatment; the second a domestic drama; and the third a sensation drama. The pieces shall be produced at the same time, and I guarantee that the success of each shall be in reverse ratio of its merits."
>
> The proposition was received with roars of laughter. Nevertheless, the three pieces were written. "Hunted Down" was the society drama; "The Long Strike" was the domestic play, and "Flying Scud" the sensation piece. They were produced simultaneously in October, 1866, and the results were precisely what Boucicault had anticipated.[9]

Although *Hunted Down* has no sensation scene, it can hardly stand on its literary merits; and, indeed, all of the three plays are basically melodramas. *Hunted Down* has another magnificently named villain in Rawdon Scudamore, but not much else. *The Long Strike* begins convincingly as a Galsworthy-like piece about a labor dispute in Manchester. Quickly, however, it degenerates into a murder melodrama. The heroine is accused of killing the villainous seducer Richard Radley, and the witness who can save her is miles away on a ship about to leave port. This situation allows Boucicault to include a scene depending on the novelty of the telegraph, just as in *The Octoroon* he had used the novelty of photography.

Flying Scud; or, A Four Legged Fortune, the broadest and most spectacular of the three, ran for 207 performances. It is a racing melodrama which brings live horses onto the stage and culminates in a horse race. Although it has been reprinted in recent years, it is really poor Boucicault. There is some ingenuity in keeping the young lovers apart; and there is some effective stage excitement in the duel scene, the fight scene, and the race. However, the characters are either so good or so evil that it is impossible to take the play seriously.

After Dark of 1868 is a puerile melodrama which steals the famous scene of the person tied to the railroad tracks from Augustin Daly's *Under the Gaslight*. However, the piece has a nice villain who uses the excellently awful pseudonym of Chandos Bellingham, and who remarks at the end of the play with a fine, "corny" theatricality: "Officer, I am Richard Knatchbull, escaped convict." The play's concluding line, spoken by a good person, is equally memorable: "You are going to the end of that crooked lane, where the guilty find their steps barred by the gates of justice."

The year 1869 was another prolific year for melodrama. *Formosa; or, The Railroad to Ruin,* which was attacked for its immorality, is a story of melodramatic intrigue about a demimondaine. This story was incongruously attached to the Oxford-Cambridge boat race, another piece of sensational staging. *Lost at Sea; or, A London Story,* which was written in collaboration with H. J. Byron, is an extremely complicated melodrama about the business world. Although it contained such scenes as a fire and a run on a bank, it failed to attract audiences. The complicated staging might be suggested by these directions for Act II, scene 3:

The Steamboat Pier at the foot of Hungerford Bridge. The pay-offices R. and L.; the River Thames at the back is seen under the space of the trestle railway. Westminster Bridge crosses the river in the distance. The opposite bank, with St. Thomas's Hospital and Lambeth Palace in the distance, is seen over Westminster Bridge, while the line of the South Embankment with its lights twinkled amid the gloom. The coloured lights over the arches of Westminster Bridge, and the railway lights and semaphores on the railway bridge, are seen. A red lamp projects from the pay-office, R. H. The clock-tower of the House of Parliament in the distance, extreme L. H.

*During the following scene, the traffic of cabs, omnibuses, wag-
gons, &c., is maintained across Westminster Bridge. The dark
form of a barge, with sail set, floats slowly up the river, it lowers
the mast to pass under the bridge. A locomotive and train passes
across the Railway Bridge above. . . .*

Elfie; or, The Cherrytree Inn of 1871 is more romantic than
many of the melodramas. It has no sensation scene, but it does
have a stage villain with the fine name of Sedley Deepcar. Its
quality might be suggested by the hero's remark to Deepcar that
"You hear the bloodhounds of the law upon your trail, and you
must wait for them to be in at the death."

Probably enough of these melodramas have been mentioned
to suggest their major characteristics and their quality. Many of
them were effective mass entertainment in their day, and many
of their devices are still used in today's entertainments. None
of them has any particular literary merit, but many have a kind of
antique charm. They do not work validly today, for we can clearly
see how they attempt to reduce the audience to a state of mass-
moronic emotionalism. However, they would probably work today as camp, for we can perceive their intentions and be amused
by their awfulness. Unfortunately, we have not yet reached that
level of perception about some of their present-day counterparts.

IV   *The Pseudo Work of Art*

Until quite recently, the modern commercial stage almost each
season produced at least one play that seemed to reach directly
to the heart of contemporary experience, a play that seemed to
sum up the essence of what we felt, a play that seemed at the time
indubitably a work of art. And yet, after the first excitement had
died and after only a little time had passed, how very false and
shoddy did many of these once meaningful documents appear.

Except for its greatest masterpieces, the drama has this quality
of trickery. A play is about a third of the length of a novel; and,
within this small space, this length of a longish short story, a play
must persuade us of the accuracy and the depth of its view. Obviously, with a length of twenty-five thousand words, all of which
must be immediately apprehensible to the dullest member of the
audience, the commercial play can be really neither very accurate
nor very profound.

A respectable number of Boucicault's plays fit into this category of the pseudo work of art. Their limitations are apparent, and we easily realize now that their glitter was only fool's gold. Still, such plays are much more respectable than the spectacular melodramas discussed in the last section. Some of them, like the best Irish plays discussed in the next chapter, have given and can still give pleasure. Their form and their worth are restricted by the limitations of the commercial stage, but they at least go as far as their limitations allow; and a few of them may be mentioned with some respect.

One of the best is *The Octoroon; or, Life in Louisiana,* which was first performed at the Winter Garden in New York on December 5, 1859, with Boucicault as Wahnotee, the Indian; Agnes Robertson, as Zoe, the octoroon; and Joseph Jefferson, as Salem Scudder. The outline of the plot is based upon Captain Mayne Reid's novel *The Quadroon,* but the accidental photographing of the murder appears to be borrowed from Albany Fonblanque's novel *The Filibuster,* while several other incidents appear to be Boucicault's own invention. The strong sense of authentic background must have been picked up by Boucicault during one of his engagements in New Orleans—mainly, no doubt, between December 1, 1855, and March 9, 1856, when he was the manager of the Gaiety Theatre in that city.

The Octoroon is one of Boucicault's most thoroughly written commercial plays. He seems to have taken more pains and given more thought to it. One proof is that he was able to treat the inflammatory question of slavery in a way that aroused the sympathies of both Northern and Southern audiences. Basically, the story concerns a Louisiana plantation which is about to be sold for debts. It has been reduced to this state by the high living of the old owner Judge Peyton, by the trickery of the former Yankee overseer Jacob M'Closky, and by the ineptness of the present Yankee overseer Salem Scudder. The judge's nephew, George, has just returned from Paris; and he falls in love with the judge's illegitimate daughter, the octoroon girl, Zoe. However, Zoe is technically a slave and must be auctioned off with the other slaves.

There are a number of melodramatic plot complications which may seem both overly complex and a bit stilted in the telling. For instance, M'Closky murders a Negro boy to obtain a letter from England that will pay off the debt; he is photographed by Scud-

der's camera in the act; a neighbor falls in love with George, who
is persuaded to propose to her in order to save the estate;
M'Closky buys Zoe at the slave auction; Wahnotee, the Indian,
is almost lynched for the murder; M'Closky is exposed, captured,
and escapes by setting fire to a river steamer; he is pursued, swim-
ming and in a canoe, by Wahnotee and finally killed in the
swamp; Zoe poisons herself.

Stated baldly and even with some incidents omitted, the plot
sounds like unadulterated hokum. However, the nature of the
drama is such that it transmutes absurdity and simplicity into the
plausible and the meaningful on the stage, and that is exactly
what happened with *The Octoroon*. What helps to keep the plot
from seeming a series of outlandish contrivances is the authentic
sense of reality that Boucicault conveys in his portrait of Southern
manners. But, even here, the reality is somewhat heightened and
sweetened. It would not be far off the mark to say that Boucicault's attitude toward his material was like the present-day attitude of Walt Disney toward his.

Certainly, a modern civil rights worker would find Boucicault's
Negroes an irritating collection of Uncle Toms. But none of them
is quite as bald a portrait as Mrs. Stowe's character, and Boucicault does not paint plantation life as totally idyllic. He notes the
hospitality given as a matter of course to the despised M'Closky,
but he also notes how Zoe is unconsciously ignored as a human
being. We may see this simultaneous criticism and appreciation
well at work in the auction scene. The most humane people are
the Southern planters, and the most vicious person is the North-
erner M'Closky. The Southerners attempt to soften the system,
but the play still says that the system is intolerable. All that we
know of Boucicault's character and dramatic practice indicate
that this full vision arose from a desire to placate all sections of
his audience. Still, however mercenary his motives, the effect suggests a more complete view of reality than usually appears in
mere entertainment.

This kowtowing to the audience may also be seen in the play's
endings. In the America of the time, the only possible way out
of the dilemma of the love story is by Zoe's death. Fortunately,
that conclusion is what is logically demanded by the moral in-
dictment of the story. In the London production, however, there
was not the public tension about miscegenation, nor was slavery

such a raw issue; and Boucicault did not hesitate to make the play more commercially attractive by substituting a happy ending in which Zoe lived to marry George. Despite this obedience to the box office, much of the play was an honest statement; and the conclusion of the American version is both inevitable and fairly tough.

The play has many elements of popular appeal cannily woven into it—a love interest, intrigue, violence, humor, a novel device in the use of photography, and a sensation scene in the burning steamboat. We cannot, incidentally, but wonder if O'Neill knew the play and used the scenes of M'Closky fleeing farther into the swamp and growing ever more frightened as the basis for the similar chase in *The Emperor Jones.*

Although none of the roles has any literary validity, there are six or eight meaty parts for actors. This difference between a theatrical character and a literary one is well suggested by the role which Boucicault elected to play himself. Wahnotee has few lines and none in English. The effect of the part rests entirely upon pantomime, and this is one quality which does not appear in a playscript. However, an experienced actor like Boucicault would never play a minor role in his own play unless he saw exceptional possibilities in it. And, according to contemporary reviewers, he scored heavily in the part.

The dialogue again raises the point of how good theatrical dialogue differs from that of fiction. A writer like Boucicault, who has an attuned and receptive ear, can get great effect from dialect. This play uses many dialects—the New England twang, the soft and slurred speech of the Southern Negro, the conventional language of wit. Actually, the dialogue is reminiscent of the orchestration of dialects that Elmer Rice later used in *Street Scene.* On the page, the dialogue appears simple and sometimes exaggerated, as for instance: "Guess they nebber was born—dem tings! what, dem?—get away! Born here—dem darkies? What, on Terrebonne! Don't b'lieve it, Mas'r George; dem black tings never was born at all; dey swarmed one mornin' on a sassafras tree in the swamp; I cotched 'em; dey ain't no 'count. Don't believe dey'll turn out niggers when dey're growed; dey'll come out sunthin' else."

Novelists as disparate as Dickens and Hawthorne have used dialogue quite as bald: for instance, the Negro dialect in *The*

House of the Seven Gables. However, for stage purposes these bald words act like musical notes. They are notations for sounds. They are hints to the actor of the dialect to be produced by his voice, and the sounds that are produced are realistic and persuasive when heard.

There is some bald and stilted dialogue in the play that no actor could greatly help—particularly some of Zoe's speeches to George. However, George's early dialogue has a fine drawing-room ease to it, and Salem Scudder's dialogue is rich in folk fancy. Actually, Boucicault has written a rich score for a full orchestra, and we cannot judge it adequately until we have heard it played—spoken on the stage. There, it was originally quite convincing. It would certainly be an error to flay Boucicault for not having written this play with the rich perfection of a Shakespeare. It would be the same kind of error that Joseph Wood Krutch made when he criticized Eugene O'Neill for having every quality of a great tragic writer except the ability to write. Krutch was making no valid criticism of drama; he was only talking about that lifeless piece of literature, the printed playscript.

It is a bit hard to arrive at a final judgment of *The Octoroon.* It worked excellently on the stage, and there are certainly good points about its theme, its characterization, its plot, and its dialogue. However, the closer one looks at these good points, the more spurious they seem. Its vitality is that of an automaton; its reality is ultimately only stage reality, an illusion, a trick. It is a more craftsman-like and accomplished trick than the bald chicaneries of *The Poor of New York* or *Flying Scud,* but it still is only a trick.

There is a little more to praise in *The Jilt.* This comedy drama is very late Boucicault and the last of his fairly accomplished commercial plays. First commercially performed in San Francisco by the Boucicault company on May 18, 1885, it is not up to the form of the early Regency comedies, having been watered down by such conventional plot excitements as a horse race, like that in *Flying Scud,* which happily concludes everything.

Despite the conventional plot, the large cast is full of appealingly and rather fully drawn characters. Boucicault's role of Myles O'Hara, the gentleman jockey, is a racy, showy Irish part; but none of the others is skimped. Sir Budleigh is a nice caricature of a burgeoning but amiable Colonel Blimp, and Phyllis Welter is one of the more charming ingenue parts of the late nineteenth-century drama. Even the minor role of her mother is keenly and truly drawn. There is a fullness and semihonesty of characterization here that is lacking in most of the commercial drama of Boucicault's maturity, and that quality comes close to redeeming the play.

Also there is a greater proportion than we found in *The Octoroon* of the wit, badinage, and repartee that was Boucicault's forte. Whenever the language tends to get too stiff, stilted, or conventional, a laugh brings it quickly back to reality. For instance:

KITTY: I have been deceived and by such a serpent.
MYLES: The first woman made the same complaint. It runs in the female family.

Or there is Myles's superbly theatrical first entrance when Kitty, rushing out of the door, plunges into his arms; and he remarks, "For what we have received, may the Lord make us truly thankful."

However, Boucicault by this time was too thoroughly a man of the commercial theater to rise much above that theater's limitations. Still, in *The Jilt* he achieved a richness which, although more theatrical than literary, was yet rich enough to remind one of the Regency comedies of his youth.

What harms most of Boucicault's commercial dramas is the intrusion of a simplified version of serious reality. There are a few plays, however, which lack this spurious caricature of real life, which are quite good, and which are still not works of art. I have in mind very broad comedies like *The Knight of Arva* and a number of canny farces. Farce is too much of a silly exaggeration of life to be considered a meaningful comment on it—which is only to say that farce is not art. Still, farce can be excellent entertainment, and it does require considerable craft.

When he wanted to, Boucicault could turn out an accomplished farce. A typical example is *Forbidden Fruit,* which was first produced at Wallack's in New York on October 3, 1876, and later at the Adelphi in London on July 3, 1880. The plot concerns how Cato Dove, a young English lawyer, is persuaded by his Senior Counsel, Mr. Sargeant Buster, to enjoy a night on the town. Dove has never since his marriage deviated one iota from the cloying embraces of his rather too sweet wife, and so he decides to join Buster in inviting two actresses to a supper party. "Actresses" is perhaps an exaggeration, for the woman attracted to Cato is Zulu, an artiste billed as The Female Cartridge because she is shot from a cannon.

Dove's attempt to fool his wife results in a series of violently incongruous situations, some of which the experienced Buster is able to release him from and some of which Buster's machinations only complicate. There is no point in relating the involved plot, but it is soundly constructed for a farce, consisting of mistaken identities, near confrontations, complexities piled on complexities, disguises, and multiple misunderstandings. The pace of the comedy must be breakneck.

Although the piece was only intended as an evening's amusement, the characters are a bit more than purely stock types, and much of the drollery of the situation rises out of how the characters, particularly Dove, react to the situation. The dialogue is for the most part fresh, terse, crisp, and undated; and some of the staging effects must have been rather attractive. In the first act, the stage is divided into two rooms; and, in the third act, it is divided into two rooms and an intervening corridor. This device was still a moderately novel one although Boucicault had used it before, and Edward Fitzball as early as 1833 in *Jonathan Bradford; or, The Murder at the Roadside Inn* had shown four rooms simultaneously. In Act II, a real horse drawing a real four-wheeled cab is brought onto the stage. In sum, this farce is still an attractive and lively one, whose effect should be largely undimmed if played today—and if a horse were available.

CHAPTER *4*

The Irish Plays

TODAY, Boucicault is mainly remembered for his three most famous Irish plays—*The Colleen Bawn, Arrah-na-Pogue*, and *The Shaughraun*. It is difficult for a sympathetic drama critic to avoid being carried away in his enthusiasm for these pieces, for they are the true stuff of theater. Their vigor, their excitement, their color, their humor are irresistible on the stage. To the colder eye of the literary critic, however, there seems a close but unavoidable distinction to be made between these Irish plays and the early Regency comedies. That distinction was probably touched upon by Boucicault himself in a letter to Marie Bancroft, referring to the Bancrofts' 1867 production of his poorly received piece *How She Loves Him*:

> I regret that my comedy was caviare to the public. I doubted its agreement with their taste and stomach and so told you before it was played.
>
> It has profited you little in money: lay by its experience.
>
> The public pretend they want pure comedy; this is not so. What they want is *domestic drama,* treated with broad, comic character. A sentimental pathetic play, comically rendered, such as *Ours, Caste, The Colleen Bawn, Arrah-na-Pogue*.
>
> Robertson differs from me, not fundamentally, but scenically; his action takes place in lodgings or drawing-rooms—mine has a more romantic scope.
>
> Be advised, then, refuse dramas which are wholly serious, wholly comic—seek those which blend the two. You have solved this very important question for yourself. Comedy, pure and simple, is rejected of 1868.[1]

This letter may be read as Boucicault's defense of the kind of play that he came to write when he turned away, in the early 1840's, from pure comedy and farce to writing popular potpourris for the commercial stage. In its most general sense, his dictum has an artistic validity. After all, Sean O'Casey—to choose but one example from many—followed it in his early Dublin tragicomedies, and created at least three masterpieces.

For Boucicault, however, the generalization was an apology for writing broadly, for writing down to the lowest common denominator of his audience, for substituting cheap emotion for deep emotion, and for adulterating his hard comic talent with large injections of pathos and thrills. Almost everything that he wrote after *Old Heads and Young Hearts* of 1844 was to accommodate his view of what would most easily please an audience. And it is within this framework of pleasing that we must judge his three best Irish plays. In them, he was trying only for entertainment and not for art. He was always working within stringent commercial limitations; consequently, much of his output must be regarded as hack work, redeemed in part only by its superior technical felicity.

Nevertheless, not all entertainment is hack work. By its very nature, entertainment does offer us only a simplified and ultimately rosy view of reality, but some entertainments are so convincingly done that we value them more warmly than we do some works of art. Such memorable entertainments as Dickens' *The Pickwick Papers,* Edmond Rostand's *Cyrano de Bergerac,* Dumas' *The Three Musketeers,* and Stevenson's *Treasure Island* are too simple in their statements to be regarded as works of art with deeply perceptive insights about man's state. Nevertheless, they are so finely done that they momentarily convince us of the rightness, the justness, and the excellence of the simplified worlds which they portray. They extract certain emotions from reality— such as romance, geniality, daring, or poetry—and build a world in which such qualities are the prime motivating emotions. Such simplified worlds, of course, are make-believe; but their narrow range of emotion proves to us, even more dramatically than do many works of art, the value of the emotions they admire. In effect, the best entertainment creates a Utopia, which is only an optimistic reminder of man's vision of the ideal.

Memorable entertainment may be distinguished from a specious piece of hack work probably by two characteristics—the degree of technical skill involved and the pervasive sincerity of the author. In the bulk of Boucicault's entertainments, we can discern only the traditional manipulations of the experienced

hack, maneuvering pasteboard figures into ever more tensely
dramatic situations. In his best entertainments, however—in the
three most popular Irish plays, in *Rip Van Winkle,* perhaps in
The Octoroon, and certainly in much of *The Jilt*—we can see both
a careful structure and a human sympathy. Both of these characteristics were apparent in the 1967 Abbey Theatre production of
The Shaughraun. The Abbey mistakenly divided Boucicault's
well-planned three-act structure into two acts, and thereby missed
some moments of intense suspense. However, in the sympathetic
playing of Conn the Shaughraun, Boucicault's own warmth, verve,
and delight in life swept compellingly over the footlights, and
laid forever the charge that he was writing about that stock
figure, the Stage Irishman. Indeed, Boucicault once defended
himself against this very charge:

> Sir, I am not surprised to read that my delineation of the Irish
> peasant provided somewhat disappointing to the Christchurch
> public—that it was found wanting in the "fire and energy" to
> which they have been accustomed. The fire and energy that con-
> sist of dancing round the stage in an expletive manner, and in-
> dulging in ridiculous capers and extravagancies of language and
> gesture, form the materials of a clowning character, known as "the
> stage Irishman," which it has been my vocation, as an artist and
> as a dramatist, to abolish. I took the Melbourne public by surprise
> at first . . . but before I left Victoria I had knocked the stuffing
> out of that old libel "Ragged Pat." If I cannot succeed in doing
> likewise here, I shall still remember Christchurch as a zoological
> garden, where the last specimen of the extinct creature is pre-
> served. In Barnum's Museum in New York I saw a "mermaid" and
> a "woolly-horse," in which the simple-minded were courted to be-
> lieve; but that Prince of Showmen never ventured to practice on
> the credulity of the public so far as to manufacture a stage Irish-
> man. He draws the line there.[2]

I Andy Blake

Andy Blake; or, The Irish Diamond (or, as it was later called,
The Dublin Boy) was first produced on March 1, 1854, at the
Boston Museum. A two-act romantic drama interlaced with
comedy, it was written as a vehicle to display Agnes' talents in
a boy's role. The piece is neither original nor, for itself, greatly
notable. The plot was taken from a French play *Le Gamin de*

Paris, but Boucicault thoroughly Irished it and, in effect, made a new play out of it.

The play's chief interest today lies in the character of Andy who is really a preliminary sketch for such later Irish heroes as Myles na Coppaleen and Conn the Shaughraun. Although a boy, Andy is already the same devil-may-care scamp that we see full-grown in the later Irish plays. He has the same engaging, easy flow of banter, jokes, and horseplay and the same basic goodness of heart. Indeed, this dual quality of being a scamp on the outside and a saint underneath is common to the best of Boucicault's Irish heroes. It is a broadening of the usual surface characteristics of most stage stereotypes and is responsible for much of the interest and excellence of his best Irish plays. This dual nature might be suggested by the following passage of banter. Superficially, Andy seems to be all jokes and fun; actually, he has just returned from rescuing a child from drowning:

MRS. BLAKE: He'll catch his death of cold. How did you get into the water, sir?
ANDY: I jumped in, to save a duck from drowning.
MULROONY: That's a physical impossibility.
ANDY: Arrah, who's talkin' of physic?
MULROONY: Buffoon denies that a duck can drown.
ANDY: Who's Buffoon, when he's at home?
MULROONY: He's dead long ago, ignoramus.
ANDY: Then how the divil could he deny that our duck didn't drown? Ignoramus yourself. Ducks has altered their minds—so has geese.
MULROONY: I should like to see a goose drown.
ANDY: Bedad, so would I. Jump into the dock wid a lookin' glass, and we'll both be satisfied.

II   The Colleen Bawn

The Colleen Bawn; or, The Brides of Garryowen, which was first produced at Laura Keene's Theatre in New York on March 29, 1860, is the most famous of Boucicault's Irish plays, although probably not quite the best. Its plot is drawn from Gerald Griffin's novel *The Collegians,* but Boucicault has made it thoroughly his own. Indeed, the play has a typical Boucicault plot, rising from excitement to excitement, complicated, with no characters wasted, but all drawn integrally into the action. The main action concerns the love affair of Hardress Cregan from the Big House and Eily O'Connor from the thatched cottage. Because of their different stations in life, Hardress conceals their marriage. When he is then driven toward another marriage and bemoans his dilemma, his devoted servant Danny Mann mistakes his meaning and thinks that his master wants him to kill Eily, the colleen bawn. In the great spectacular scene of the play, Danny takes the girl out onto the lake and pushes her in. At that moment, the gay scamp of a poacher, Myles na Coppaleen, appears; shoots Danny; and dives headlong into the lake to save Eily. It would be difficult to top the theatrical excitement of this scene, but Boucicault manages to do so with the abortive wedding scene of Act III, in which the appropriate boy gets the appropriate girl, and the villains get their appropriate rewards.

There are a few melodramatic improbabilities about the plot, such as Anne Chute's mistaking Kyrle Daly for Hardress Cregan, and Mrs. Cregan's tricking of Danny Mann with the glove. In the liveliness of performance, however, these improbabilities are less noticeable than they are on the page. Although we may criticize Boucicault for resorting to them, we could probably also criticize Shakespeare for the artificial business of the handkerchief in *Othello,* or Ibsen for the trite old device of the letter in *A Doll's House.*

We can probably also give Boucicault a good modicum of half-praise for his characterization. He does give some of the characters enough individuality to draw them away from the complete stereotype. For instance, Eily O'Connor, the Colleen Bawn (or fair-haired girl), is essentially a Black-eyed Susan—a dewy-eyed, sweet, faithful, and inconquerably virtuous ingenue. Still, Boucicault gives Eily a couple of touches that hint at an individuality which Susan and dozens of her sister-characters do not have. For one thing, Eily has an engaging lack of education; and Hardress attempts to correct her pronunciation and make it more acceptably Anglo-Irish. This imperfection does not make her, however, less appealing; if anything, it heightens her charm.

Anne Chute, the secondary heroine from the Big House, has a suggestion of fullness perhaps beyond Eily's. She is, to use the title of Lady Morgan's novel, the Wild Irish Girl. She has considerable spirit and vivacity and rather more wit than most women characters since Sheridan and Goldsmith. For example, we have some of her banter in the first scene of Act I:

MRS. CREGAN: . . . Show Mr. Corrigan here. . . . I hate this man; he was my husband's agent, or what the people here call a middle-man—vulgarly polite, and impudently obsequious.

HARDRESS: Genus squireen—a half sir, and a whole scoundrel.

ANNE: I know—a potato on a silver plate: I'll leave you to peel him. Come, Mr. Daly, take me for a moonlight walk, and be funny.

KYRLE: Funny, ma'am, I'm afraid I am—

ANNE: You are heavy, you mean; you roll through the world like a hogshead of whiskey; but you only want tapping for pure spirits to flow out spontaneously. Give me your arm. Hold that glove now. You are from Ballinasloe, I think?

KYRLE: I'm Connaught to the core of my heart.

ANNE: To the roots of your hair, you mean. I bought a horse at Ballinasloe fair that deceived me; I hope you won't turn out to belong to the same family.

KYRLE: What did he do?

ANNE: Oh! like you, he looked well enough—deep in the chest as a pool—a-dhiol, and broad in the back as the Gap of Dunloe—but after two days' warm work he came all to pieces, and Larry, my groom, said he'd been stuck together with glue.

In her serious moments, Anne does sink back into the stock diction of the conventional nineteenth-century heroine, but there is still much more in her than in the stock heroines of Douglas Jerrold and Bulwer-Lytton. There is enough suggestion of personality to help an actress build an individual rather than merely to exist as a piece of mobile stage architecture.

Boucicault has skimped none of the women. Even the minor characters of Mrs. Cregan and Sheelah Mann have their big scenes. In a short scene with Anne in Act III, the actress who plays Mrs. Cregan has a moment in which she can excellently tear passion to tatters. Danny's mother, Sheelah, has an impressive moment also in Act III when she is caught by the soldiers. Her language and her emotion ring true here.

The men have even better acting roles, and I will discuss just four of them. Hardress Cregan is not the best acting part: he can never run away with the show, but his is the most complicated character. He is the character who most fully contains some real contradictions. He is torn between his West Briton, Anglo-Irish background and his love for the Irish-Irish Eily. These feelings are sometimes expressed rather stiltedly, but Boucicault does deviate from the hero-purer-than-the-driven-snow, and makes Hardress at times feel, if not a contempt, at least a shame for Eily and her background. He is not a memorable individual, but we can class him with the Alfred Evelyn of Bulwer-Lytton's *Money* and with the Peg Woffington of the Taylor-Reade *Masks and Faces* as certainly more than the flat stage character. Hardress has a dilemma which comes not from the finagling of the plot, but from contrary desires in himself; and, when a playwright draws such a character, he is heading in the direction of art.

The old priest, Father Tom, is interesting. The modern stereotype of the priest seems most often copied from the old canon of Paul Vincent Carroll's *The White Steed,* and he is familiar to the modern audience in the cinema stereotype of Barry Fitzgerald. This stereotype is an innocuous whitewashing that leaves one or two appealing human crotchets to make the character human and lovable. In contrast, the much more human priests of novelist J. F. Powers do have real faults of character, and putting on a cassock does not absolve them from being human beings. Boucicault's Father Tom leans a bit more to Powers than to the stereotype. He has been stripped of his parish by his bishop; he is an upright and sympathetic man; and he has a lovely drinking scene with Myles and Eily and Sheelah, which displays his wit and humor and humanity. His comment as he superintends the making of the punch reads:

> See now, my children, there's a moral in everything, e'en in a jug of punch. There's the sperrit, which is the sowl and strength of the man. (*Myles pours spirit from the keg*) That's the whiskey. There's the sugar, which is the smile of woman; (*Eily puts sugar*) without that, life is without taste or sweetness. Then there's the lemon, (*Eily puts lemon*) which is love; a squeeze now and again does a boy no harm; but not too much. And the hot water (*Sheelah pours water*) which is adversity—as little as possible if ye plaze—that makes the good things better still.

This whole little scene, which ends with the singing of "Cruiskeen Lawn," is a theatrically delightful interlude. If we remember the fine "hooley" in the second act of *Juno and the Paycock,* we might think that the effect of Boucicault's scene was not lost upon Sean O'Casey.

Danny Mann and Myles-na-Coppaleen (Myles of the little horses) are the really meaty parts in the play. Both have some claim to literary merit, and both are grand acting parts in the same way that Mercutio is one. To be traditional about it, both are opposite halves of the traditional role of the hero's servant, which goes back at least to Roman comedy. Myles is the sunny comic servant, but Danny is a really black role. This slavishly doglike fidelity to his master Hardress was actually no mere study in individual psychology. Michael J. Molloy in his brilliant play *The King of Friday's Men* draws a similar character, and he makes the point that this was definitely an Irish type. Boucicault does, however, give a hint of dark psychology here, of the blighted being, the hunchback. A bald and pure melodrama would show such a character as a study in motiveless malignancy, but Boucicault's every touch is to humanize Danny. Like Hardress, Danny has his human contradictions; he is conscious of right and wrong, but his fidelity to his master overpowers his conscience fairly easily, and there is only something of a balance in his deathbed scene. There we get a kind of racking agony because of his awareness of the contradictions pulling at him.

Myles has no internal dilemmas like Hardress or Danny, although in him there is the same duality that we noted in Andy Blake. He is something of a scalliwag on the outside and a noble fellow underneath. Although none of the other characters is skimped, Myles is given an opportunity for bravura acting, for an actor to score in a big way. He is raised above the stereotype of the faithful servant by many touches—by his quick wit, his ability at repartee, his ebullience, and by the hint that he is a poacher and something of a rogue. Actually, in Myles we get an Irish version of the lovable rogue that we see also in Falstaff or in Long John Silver. He rises by wit against the adversity of his social position and nearly always lands on his feet. To this extent, then, because of the fine things lavished upon him by Boucicault, he becomes much fuller than the usual broth-of-a-bhoy stage Irishman.

There is a hint, just a hint, of a real theme in the dilemma facing Hardress and Eily. There were two classes of people living in Ireland—the people of the Big House and those in the white-washed hovel. Boucicault never honestly comes to grips with this theme, however; instead, he resolves his problem by a happy ending and a marriage. In other words, the theme is roman-ticized as, indeed, the whole picture of Ireland in this play is. There is a hint of realism here and there, of a true picture of Irish life; but largely Boucicault selected only the happy things and left out the poverty and the squalor and the hatred and the injustice. A real-life marriage between an Eily O'Connor and a scion of the Big House, in which love conquers all and topples over the social barriers, is the most hopeless romanticism. What a pity, for here was the first dramatist really to turn to Irish life for his subject, and he used that subject for mere entertainment. He used it dishonestly. He Walt-Disneyed it up for public con-sumption. Boucicault had stumbled on a real subject, and he had enough talent to have mined it. However, he was a businessman of the theater, and well aware that an Irish Lower Depths would have failed at the box office. It would be forty years more before a John Synge, a Padraic Colum, and a Lady Gregory turned to Irish life as a subject for a work of art.

III Arrah-na-Pogue

Arrah-na-Pogue follows fairly closely the successful formula of *The Colleen Bawn*. Produced in its original version at the old Theatre Royal, Hawkins Street, Dublin, on November 7, 1864, it has, like the earlier piece, two sets of young lovers. One pair is conventional, and the other is composed of a spirited Irish girl and a laughing scamp of a hero. There is again an unspeakable worm of a villain, a glossily bland view of the Irish problem, and an effective use of local color, with scenes set in such attrac-tive places in County Wicklow as Glendalough and the Devil's Glen. The gay conviviality of *The Colleen Bawn's* punch-making scene is considerably expanded in the long scene of the wedding party which concludes Act I. This eminently theatrical scene utilizes song, dance, color, and stage movement beautifully. There are fiddlers, a piper, a lovely jig or two, a droll dancing contest, and Boucicault's own new words to "The Wearing of the Green," as sung by the hero, Shaun the Post.

There is a deftly handled romantic and melodramatic plot

which contains an excellent comic trial that Shaw seems to have had in mind when writing the trial scene in *The Devil's Disciple*. There is also a fine, climactic sensation scene in which the condemned Shaun escapes from his cell, scales an ivy-covered tower, and rescues Arrah from the clutches of that slimy process server, Michael Feeny. This is a complex business to stage, but well worth the attempt.

The characterization is, for the most part, no great improvement over that of *The Colleen Bawn*. The romantic hero and heroine are flat types whose speech is stiltedly conventional. Michael Feeny is a totally contemptible wretch, quite on the lines of the Half-Sir of the earlier play. The peasant heroine, Arrah-na-Pogue (Arrah of the kiss), has a bit of Anne Chute's fine playfulness in the first act, but becomes finally a stock figure of suffering as Boucicault, fattening his own role, more and more allows her lover Shaun the Post to upstage her.

Shaun is the Myles na Coppaleen figure of the play; and his fidelity, self-sacrifice, and courage could easily have been nauseatingly overdrawn. However, Boucicault makes these qualities palatable and almost plausible, by weaving into them Shaun's other qualities—a fine zest for life, a surpassing geniality, and a glib gift of banter. Shaun is no real person, but he is a showy stage part that in the hands of a good actor like Boucicault would take on a moving stage reality. The other notable role is Colonel Bagenal O'Grady, the unsuccessful rival for Fanny Power's hand. The O'Grady has altogether more dash than Beamish Mac Coul, the nominal hero who wins the girl; and he also has a few nicely humanizing touches of wit.

Although the piece is not to my mind quite up to *The Colleen Bawn*, its greatest virtue is that it is so much more "written" than Boucicault's usual claptrap farces, melodramas, and adaptations. In such plays, he often harms a potentially tolerable scene by giving it only a few cursory and inadequate lines. In *Arrah-na-Pogue*, however, he lingers over most of his scenes lovingly, and he develops them fully. When he took the time to do it, Boucicault could always write fine comic dialogue. In this play, he does take the time, and he produces several excellently droll and genial scenes.

Probably the comic trial of Shaun is the most quoted example of the play's humor, and even Shaw did it the compliment of

using it as a model. However, the scene in Dublin Castle when
Beamish, Fanny, and the O'Grady all arrive separately to plead
for Shaun's life is neatly witty itself. And, though not a witty
scene, the party of Act I offers a blueprint for high spirits that
could hardly miss fire in an adequate production. As one brief
example of this contagious good humor, there is the play's second
scene in which both Shaun and Arrah are first introduced:

SHAUN: This is my weddin' mornin'; sure my breast is so big wid my
    heart this minit, that I feel like a fowl wid her first egg. Egorra,
    and this same love brings a man out in a fine perspiration, long
    life to it. And there's Arrah's cabin; the oysther-shell that's got the
    pearl of my heart in it. I wonder is she awake. (*Knocks*) No signs
    of the chimney anyway. Arrah, suilis! Arrah, mo millia storeen!
    If you are slapin' don't answer me; but if you are up, open the
    dure softly. (*He sings through the keyhole*)

> Open the dure softly,
> Somebody wants ye, dear;
> Give me a chink no wider than
> You'll fill up wid your ear.
> Or, if you're hard of hearing, dear,
> Your mouth will do as well;
> Just put your lips agan the crack,
> And hear what I've to tell.
> Open the dure, softly,
> Somebody wants you, dear.

(*Arrah opens the window*)

ARRAH: Hur-rrosh! hoo! that porkawn has got loose again, the ma-
    rauder!
SHAUN: Is it the pig she takes me for?
ARRAH (*Aside*): It's that thief o' the world, Shaun. (*Aloud*) Or is it
    the ould cow that's broke her sugaun? (*Calls*) Coop, coop, coop!
SHAUN: Another baste! Have I been singin' to the ould mare till I've
    got a quadruped voice?
ARRAH (*Aside*): Where is he hidin'? I'll take a peep. (*She puts out
    her head; he catches her round the neck*) Oh, murther! who's
    that?
SHAUN: It's the pig that's got loose.
ARRAH: Let me go, Shaun! D'ye hear me, sir? let me go!
SHAUN: First I'll give ye the coward's blow. Come here, ye vagabone,
    till I hit ye undher the nose wid my mouth.[3]

Of course, this is sentimental stage-Irish, but it is also theatrically charming. And perhaps, more generally, that is a fair judgment of the play. As literature, *Arrah-na-Pogue* has little standing. It is a cartoon rather than a portrait, an entertainment rather than a work of art. Still, it is such a droll, good-humored, and even exciting piece that one must like it. It is *Kitsch*, but endearing *Kitsch*.

IV The Shaughraun

The Shaughraun, whose title may be translated from Gaelic as "The Wanderer," was first produced on November 14, 1874, at Wallack's Theatre in New York. It is the finest of Boucicault's best-known Irish plays, but it probably does not require a lengthy analysis, for it is cut from quite the same cloth as *The Colleen Bawn* and *Arrah-na-Pogue*. The cutting, however, is more skillful—so skillful, in fact, that the piece might be taken as an example of how close entertainment at its best can approach to art. Indeed, I am inclined to think that *The Shaughraun* may take as secure a place in minor dramatic literature as *London Assurance*, if not *Old Heads and Young Hearts*.

The play has the literary faults of Boucicault's other crowd-pleasing entertainments, but those faults are so camouflaged by the virtues that they seem small blots on the page and should seem nearly invisible on the stage. One of the faults is the usual Boucicaultian melodramatic plot with lots of ruses, escapes, and thrilling moments. However, this melodramatic plot has such a fertility of fine scenes and such a neatly structured building up to its great moments that its implausibility might certainly be overlooked on the stage because of its compelling theatricality.

The brilliant Abbey Theatre production of the play thoroughly emphasized this point. The rare moments in which Boucicault resorted to the more hackneyed conventions of the nineteenth-century stage were almost lost in the succession of brilliant situations. One of these situations, the wake scene with the keeners wailing over the body of the presumably dead Shaughraun, is undoubtedly among the most effective comic scenes ever penned by an Irish dramatist. But, even in the melodramatic scenes, Boucicault rose to moments of convincing reality. In the last act, for instance, when the enraged peasants turn on the informer, his anguish, as he debates whether to face them or to leap off the cliff, is intensely impressive.

However, the really redeeming features of the play are the pervasive geniality of the dialogue, the fine fullness with which (even more than in *Arrah-na-Pogue*) the scenes are developed, and above all the constant playful humor which Boucicault could do so masterfully. One example of how this playful humor overcomes the theatrical stereotype is the character of Captain Molineux, the young English officer who falls in love with Claire Ffolliott, the sister of the outlawed Irish gentleman, Robert Ffolliott. Actually, there are three pairs of lovers: Claire and Molineux, Robert and Arte O'Neal, and Moya and Conn the Shaughraun. Robert and Arte are fairly conventional, romantic straight parts; but Claire and Molineux are considerably more. Claire is a spirited Irish girl rather like Anne Chute, and Molineux is the well-intentioned but very English beau. Boucicault gets, then, in the charming interplay between Molineux Englishness and Claire's Irishness, a *John Bull's Other Island, in petto.*[4] For instance:

MOLINEUX: My good girl.
CLAIRE: So to you. (*Aside*) He takes me for the dairymaid.
MOLINEUX: Is this place called Swillabeg?
CLAIRE: No; it is called Shoolabeg.
MOLINEUX: Beg pardon; your Irish names are so unpronounceable. You see, I'm an Englishman.
CLAIRE: I remarked your misfortune. Poor creature, you couldn't help it.
MOLINEUX: I do not regard it as a misfortune.
CLAIRE: Got accustomed to it, I suppose. Were you born so?
MOLINEUX: Is your mistress at home?
CLAIRE: My mistress. Oh, 'tis Miss O'Neal you mane!
MOLINEUX: Delicious brogue—quite delicious! Will you take her my card?
CLAIRE: I'm afeard the butter will spoil if I lave it now.
MOLINEUX: What is your pretty name?
CLAIRE: Claire! What's yours?
MOLINEUX: Molineux—Captain Molineux. Now, Claire, I'll give you a crown if you will carry my name to your mistress.
CLAIRE: Will you take my place at the churn while I go?
MOLINEUX: How do you work the infernal thing? (*Crosses to her*)
CLAIRE: Take hould beside me, and I'll show you. (*He takes handle*

of churn beside her, they work together) There, that's it! Beautiful! You were intended for a dairymaid!

MOLINEUX: I know a dairymaid that was intended for me.

CLAIRE: That speech only wanted a taste of the brogue to be worthy of an Irishman.

MOLINEUX: (*Kissing her*): Now I'm perfect.

CLAIRE (*Starting away*): What are you doing?

MOLINEUX: Tasting the brogue. Stop, my dear; you forget the crown I promised you. Here it is. (*He hands her the money*) Don't hide your blushes, they become you.

CLAIRE: Never fear—I'll be even wid your honour yet. Don't let— (*up to porch*)—the butther spoil while I'm gone. (*Going, and looking at card*) What's your name again—Mulligrubs?

MOLINEUX: No; Molineux.

CLAIRE: I ax your pardon. You see I'm Irish, and the English names are so unpronounceable. (*Exit house*)

The play has such a large amount of similar dialogue that its stock characters become genuinely broadened and humanized, while even the most exciting twists of plot seem less outlandish and implausible than those of *The Colleen Bawn* and *Arrah-na-Pogue*. If Boucicault had stuck to his genius for humor, he might well have given us more than a slim handful of plays for our literature.

Probably the only other point that needs to be made about the play is that the star part of Conn the Shaughraun is one of the great acting roles of the nineteenth century. Conn is, of course, a blood brother of Andy Blake and Boucicault's other Irish heroes, but he is infinitely better than that genial noble peasant Shaun the Post or even than the redoubtable Myles na Coppaleen. He has all of their virtues, but he has in much more pronounced fashion the qualities of the playboy. Boucicault describes him as "the soul of every fair, the life of every funeral, the first fiddle at all weddings and patterns." There is a magnificent vitality to Conn that comes out in his zest for drinking and poaching and love-making. And there is a very endearing Huckleberry Finn quality in his intention to continue drinking, poaching, and love-making no matter how much society tries to restrict him. Conn's irrepressible vitality and his equally irrepressible wit are probably best shown in the brilliant wake scene which suggests that nothing, not even death, can keep Conn down. However, we can also

see a bit of both qualities in this brief exchange between Conn
and his mother:

CONN (*Entering with a paper in his hand*): There's writing upon it.
   Himself has sent me a letther. Well, this is the first I ever got,
   and well to be sure, (*looks at it—turns it over*) I'd know more
   about it if there was nothing in it; but it's the writin' bothers me.
MRS. O'KELLY (*Entering*): Is that yourself, Conn?
CONN (*Aside*): I wish it was somebody else that had book larnin'.
MRS. O'KELLY: What have you there?
CONN: It's a letther the masther is afther writin' to me.
MRS. O'KELLY: What's in it?
CONN: Tuppence was in it for postage. (*Aside*) That's all I made out
   of it.
MRS. O'KELLY: I mane what does he say in it?
CONN: Rade it!
MRS. O'KELLY: You know I can't.
CONN: Oh, ye ignorant ould woman!
MRS. O'KELLY: I know I am; but I took care to send you to school,
   Conn, though the sixpence a week it cost me was pinched out of
   my stomach and off my back.
CONN: The Lord be praised that ye had it to spare, anyway.
MRS. O'KELLY: Go on, now—it's makin' fun of yer ould mother ye
   are. Tell me what the young masther says.
CONN: In the letther?
MRS. O'KELLY: Yes!
CONN (*Aside*): Murther, what'll I do? (*Aloud*) Now, mind it's a
   secret. (*Reads*) "Collee costhum garanga caravat selibubu luckli
   rastuck pig."
MRS. O'KELLY: What's that—it's not English!
CONN: No; it's in writin'—now kape that to yourself.

There is a charmingly humorous interplay of character and situation here, and the whole play is full of such scenes. It is so full
that it almost transcends its conventional plotting, its basically
stereotyped characters, and its romantic simplification of real life.
Conn, in other words, is so good that we forget *The Shaughraun's*
faults.

V *The Minor Irish Plays*

Individual Irish characters figure importantly in many Boucicault plays; and the old servant in *Kerry,* Conor the Rash in *The*

Knight of Arva, and Myles O'Hara in *The Jilt* are only a few of the most notable. However, Boucicault wrote only a few completely Irish plays, ones peopled mainly by Irish characters and set in Ireland. In addition to the three most popular ones which we have already discussed, perhaps five others should be briefly mentioned. None of them is up to the standard of *The Colleen Bawn, Arrah-na-Pogue,* or *The Shaughraun;* and most of them tend to be baldly and blatantly commercial.

For instance, *The Rapparee; or, The Treaty of Limerick,* which was originally produced in September, 1870, at the Princess Theatre in London, is a three-act romantic drama set around the end of the seventeenth century. It contains large doses of spectacle and melodrama which are unleavened by Boucicault's saving humor. The emotions of the characters are only stage ones, and the dialogue is little more than a patchwork of theatrical clichés. Here, for example, is Grace O'Hara, the heroine, speaking to Ulick M'Murragh, the villain: "I fear not to speak the truth. I come from a love-tryst with the Rapparee! His kisses glow upon my cheek, his love-words sing within mine ear! He has rejected with scorn the treason that you leapt at—he would not forget his honor, not for all the love I feel for him!"

On March 17, 1873, Boucicault opened an engagement at Booth's Theatre in New York with *Daddy O'Dowd; or, Turn About Is Fair Play* (later called *The O'Dowd; or, Life in Galway,* and still later called *Suil-a-Mor; or, Life in Galway*). This play is considerably better than *The Rapparee,* and the title role gave Dion an effective old man's part. A four-act drama, the action is set partly in London and partly in Galway, and its plot is based on *Les Crochets du Père Martin* by Corman and Grangé. The plot which Boucicault borrowed from the French is full of coincidence and artificial contrivance, and Boucicault has added to it large injections of sentiment and melodrama. There are some local-color touches which ring true and which suggest some first-hand knowledge of the Claddagh fishermen and of Connemara and Galway. There is also a note of patriotism that seems genuine, despite its stock phrasing. Portions of the dialogue and bits of characterization have a fluent persuasiveness, but, over-all, a tawdry conventionality dominates the play, and it reads as if it were a rush job.

The Amadan, written late in Boucicault's career and never

published, was first produced in 1883; but it was not popular on the stage despite one or two spectacular effects. A few critics who have read the manuscript have admired it, but the piece seems to me basically a tangled and tedious contrivance resting on such tired devices as scraps of paper and discoveries of old deeds.

Robert Emmet is also a late play and was a revision of an uncompleted script Frank Marshall had originally written for Sir Henry Irving. The Boucicault company presented it on November 5, 1884, at the McVicker's Theatre in Chicago; but it was produced on the day of a Presidential election and ran for only three nights. Tolson feels that the play reads well, but it seems to me vitiated by a stock patriotism that never rises to true eloquence. Its quality may be suggested by its conclusion when Emmet, about to be executed, embraces his friend Norman and says:

> This for Sarah, and this for Tiney. (*Kisses him twice farewell. He goes up L. C. to the wall of the prison; stands a moment as if in prayer, then pressing the medallion to his lips, he extends his left arm in which he holds his cravat.*) God bless my country! (*He drops the cravat; a volley is heard; he falls on his knees, his hand on his heart; the shots strike the wall, and show where they have scarred the masonry. Small clouds of dust fall to the ground. The black flag is raised. Bell tolls. Stage dark. Norman stands with his head averted. The wall behind Emmet slowly opens. A vista of pale blue clouds appears. The figure of Ireland clothed in palest green and with a coronet of shamrocks in her hair descends slowly; and bending forward when she reaches the spot behind Emmet, she kneels. Two children at her feet, R. and L., draw slowly back the body of Emmet until his head lies looking up into her face.*)
>
> TABLEAU

Boucicault's last Irish play was *The Spae Wife*, or, as it was later called, *Cuishla Ma Chree*. First commercially presented on February 20, 1888, at the Hollis Street Theatre in Boston, it failed there and in Chicago. The piece has not been published, but it was an Irish version of Scott's *Guy Mannering*. A Boston reviewer remarked of it: "It is insufferably slow at times, and throughout has a fatal lack of vivacity and interest. . . . Many

of the situations are good, but several are weak. . . . The dialogue in most positions is commonplace, having little of the
flavor of Boucicault's wit and brightness. Occasionally there are
flashes of brilliancy . . . but these are but beads strung on a
cheap, spun twine." 5

And that, of course, is what is wrong with all of Boucicault's
Irish plays: they are beads, sometimes brilliant and sometimes
tawdry; but always strung on a cheap commercial twine. It is
remarkable that, working within the limitations of commercial
dramaturgy, Boucicault could three times pass off this paste as
the real stuff of life and literature. We realize later that we have
been taken in, but it is most remarkable that in the case of *The
Shaughraun* at least we do not mind.

CHAPTER *5*

The Influence of Boucicault

B OUCICAULT spent fifty active, arduous, and often brilliantly successful years in the theater. He was for much of this time one of the best-known and most outspoken authors, actors, and managers in the English-speaking theater. His ideas, methods, and innovations were noted with respect. Literally dozens of notable actors have testified to his excellence as both actor and director. Among the literary men, Mark Twain, Bret Harte, Charles Reade, and Oscar Wilde—to mention but a few—sought out his opinions or his aid. Indeed, there seems such an endless amount of testimony that one hardly knows where to begin or what to select from the seemingly endless number of often fascinating details.

For instance, it is a little-known fact that E. A. Sothern's famous performance as Lord Dundreary in *Our American Cousin* owed something to his friend Boucicault. As T. Edgar Pemberton remarked, "This was the performance that made Dundreary whiskers and Dundreary coats famous, but the original long frock coat used by Sothern was borrowed from Boucicault." [1] Details such as this could probably be cited until this volume became twice its length, but perhaps the best way to approach the matter is to consider in the most general terms Boucicault's influence on acting, stage directing, theatrical management, and, above all, playwriting.

I *On Acting*

In 1882, Boucicault gave a lecture at the Lyceum Theatre in London on the art of acting. His remarks, although generally sound, are rather rudimentary. Despite their basic nature, they do indicate experience, canniness, and how deeply Boucicault was

immersed in the nineteenth-century tradition of acting. His strictures, for instance, on diction and walking seem sound but mainly
for straight roles and stock acting. A rather ludicrous limitation
appears in the remarks on diction, for his own was far from
clipped British stage purity. Indeed, there is one account of the
lecture that shows how amusing his broguing mispronunciations
were to some members of the audience.

Despite these reservations, some of Boucicault's generalizations
about stage movement, enunciation, and external analysis rather
than soulful empathy into a role seem eminently on the side of
the gods. Some of the remarks about movement put him most
definitely as a post-T. W. Robertson realistic actor. He deplored,
for instance, the highly theatrical exit, in which an actor says,
"Now, I am going," and then crosses the length of the stage, turns,
delivers his parting lines with a flourish, and exits presumably to
a round of milked applause. His convention of realism is not
quite ours—that is, Marlon Brando playing Stanley Kowalski
would not have regarded Boucicault's Conn the Shaughraun as a
realistic study. Still, for its own day, Boucicault's style of acting
gave the impression of holding the mirror up to nature; and that
is all that Brando's style does too.

Boucicault's best remarks on acting are contained in a handful
of articles written toward the end of his life. In one or two instances, he seems to contradict himself; but, generally, his
thoughts are provocative. He is mainly interested in the question
of whether the "mimetic art is a craft, an artistic process, or an
effusion, an ecstasy." This is a debate that still goes on, and we
have seen it recently in the proselytization of American, neo-
Stanislavskian or "Method" actors.

Boucicault's comments on the subject make a great deal of
sense. He begins quite justly by noting that acting is not all of
a piece. He sees a distinct difference between tragic and comic
acting. To him, comedy imitates the weaknesses of people. It
notes the distinction between individuals, "and it is exhibited by
the *manner* in which each bears and expresses his or her trouble,
or deals with his neighbors." [2] To him, tragedy portrays the
passions to which strong natures are subject, and "strong natures
exhibit no distinctive character. Heroes are monotonous. Othello,
Richard, Macbeth, Lear, Hamlet, are great sufferers from various

causes, but they suffer alike; they all cry in the same histrionic key." [3]

Such disparate types, then, as the comic and tragic require different styles of acting. The acting of comedy "is largely a physiological study, tragedy is largely pathologic." To portray the mannerisms symptomatic of comic character defects, a comic actor must have his voice, his whole body, in perfect control. He must know the inflection, the posture, the gesture, the gait which convey his character's essence; and he must be able quite consciously to imitate them and to repeat the imitations at will. The tragic actor is no such external critic, but he must at least sometime have felt an empathy with the character.

Yet even here Boucicault has some reservations about feeling, the "fine phrenzy" or the "psychic spasm" of the tragic actor. First, he notes that some tragic figures, such as the popular Louis XI of Delavigne, must be treated at least partially from the outside, for a part of their makeup is "comic"—which is to say that in part they are character roles. His second reservation is particularly telling. What happens, he wonders, to the "psychic spasm" when the tragic actor repeats a role for two hundred nights? Most theatrical criticisms of acting are of the inspired first nights rather than the tired and mechanical two hundredth. As any actor knows, the repetition of any role becomes a mechanical process. Boucicault remarks:

> If any person will undertake to repeat a speech a great number of times he will find that, after a certain number, the sense of what he is talking about will fade, and subsequently the words will come involuntarily while he is thinking of something else. It has occurred to me, after playing a part for two or three hundred times, to find myself uttering the words, using the expression of face and all the artistic movements, without the slightest consciousness of what I am doing or saying, my mind being elsewhere. Some person would enter the theatre on whom I desired to make a favorable impression by the performance, and I would address myself attentively to my business. The words would leave me. To recover them I was obliged to remove my mind from attempting to remember, fix it on some other subject, and the mechanical memory would be restored. So it is with the tragedian who has appeared a thousand times in *Hamlet;* it is physically

impossible for his mind to act otherwise than mechanically after a certain time! [4]

Just as telling is his droll account of a great actress playing Constance in Shakespeare's *King John,* "with her breast heaving with simulated emotion, her voice tremulous, and tears streaming from her eyes. . . ." At the same time, she is infuriated by a crying child in the audience and interjects in her speech such asides to the prompter as, "I shall break down if that squeaker is not choked by somebody." She got, remarks Boucicault, a whirlwind of applause; and "During her passional scene I failed to detect any lack of tenderness in her voice. Her face was full of the feeling with which she was supposed to be overwhelmed." [5]

Boucicault does not advocate a totally brainless and mechanical technique. He feels that personality must color any role done well, but that personality without technique is as bad as frenzied feeling without technique. "Nearly every woman has the nervous faculty of making a hysterical fool of herself. Some men have the same power; for the artistic mind, being incubative, is in a large degree—female. If you waggle your finger before the eyes of a bird placed on his back, he will be comatised!—and so, many artists waggle their fingers before their own eyes, and think their giddiness is inspiration!" [6]

He does not quite say that acting "is a purely artistic process" uninspired by "a fine phrenzy," but, as his painstaking drill of young actors in Palmer's school showed, he thought it a "vain pretense that acting is an effusion uncontrolled by art." And that emphasis on technique seems a most salutary view.

II   On Stage Direction

Although the Greek dramatists are said to have drilled the chorus, taught the actors, and been in near total control of a performance, the stage director as we now know him was only beginning to come into his own in the nineteenth century. Actors were usually just given their "sides" to memorize and then came to rehearsal where someone or other in the company in a rather perfunctory way placed them about on the stage. If the placing were done by the leading actor, the others were liable to be quite considerably out of the limelight. A number of nineteenth-century theater men—such as Macready, T. W. Robertson, and Boucicault —began, however, to view the production of a play as a matter demanding a much closer, more meticulous attention. W. S. Gilbert, a fanatically painstaking director, even asserted that Robertson "invented stage-management":

> It was an unknown art before his time. Formerly, in a conversation scene, for instance, you simply brought down two or three chairs from the flat and placed them in a row in the middle of the stage, and then people sat down and talked, and when the conversation was ended the chairs were replaced. Robertson showed how to give life and variety and nature to the scene by breaking it up with all sorts of little incidents and delicate by-play. I have been at many of his rehearsals and learnt a great deal from them.[7]

George Rowell more justly says that "In the field of spectacular drama Boucicault had already asserted the claim of the author to control the rehearsals of his own play. Now Robertson applied that control to the rehearsal of drawing-room drama, and since, unlike Boucicault, he did not appear in his own plays, he was able to give greater attention to ensemble and balance."[8] Of course, some of Boucicault's own works were drawing-room plays; but Rowell is quite correct in the rest of his statement.

The more impressive effect of these meticulously directed plays of Boucicault and Robertson did not go unnoticed. Gilbert, Pinero, and Shaw followed their lead; and later Granville-Barker, although an author, became a superb director of other people's plays. The stage was set for the twentieth-century stage director who was not the author or the leading actor, but only a director.

Boucicault had about thirty-five years of nearly constant work in stage direction, which made him certainly one of the most experienced workers in the field. He must have conducted between five and ten thousand rehearsals. His canniness as a director is indicated by the frequent long runs of his plays, and many of these plays required effects as difficult and dazzling as, say, those in Lionel Bart's *Blitz*. Perhaps two comments may suggest his chief qualities and faults as a director. In the season of 1861–62, Squire Bancroft was playing at the Theatre Royal in Birmingham, and of this time he later remarked:

I remember, too, being called upon to play the Counsel for the Defense in Dion Boucicault's drama, *The Trial of Effie Deans*. The part, although appearing only in the trial scene, was very important, being played in London by the author of the *Colleen Bawn* himself, who came down for the final rehearsal. The Dion Boucicault I am alluding to is not, of course, my dear friend the present bearer of the name, but his father. When I was half-way through the scene, Boucicault whom I then met for the first time, came quietly to me and said, "You are all wrong about this part, my dear fellow; let me rehearse the rest of the scene for you. I can see your intelligence, and I fancy you will grasp my view of it directly." I thanked him for his kindness, and after rehearsal went away to model my performance entirely upon his, for I saw at once how right he was, and how wrong I had been. The result was a considerable success on my part, the credit of which was due to one half-hour with Boucicault.[9]

Added to this comment upon Boucicault's tactful and exact ability to demonstrate what he wanted, should be this account by the Boston actress Kate Ryan:

On the other hand stands Dion Boucicault. How we dreaded his return! He was a martinet, but as a stage director he was invaluable. He had a way of changing his ideas at each rehearsal, and while they were always good, they were somewhat perplexing. I remember once, when uncertain just where to go on the stage, I went where he had planned an imaginary table. He shrieked: "Are you going to walk over that table?"

I was confused and stepped aside quickly.

"Here, here, don't run about like a hen with its head cut off!"

It was his delight to get the women of the company confused to the extent of shedding bitter tears. It is told of him that a member of his company who was painstaking, but whom Mr. Boucicault had selected as a special target to shoot at, ventured to say, when the director reprimanded him for some business on the stage: "Mr. Boucicault, I have written the directions as you gave them to me yesterday."

"Ah!" said Boucicault in his Dublin brogue and sweetest manner, "yesterday, certainly, my boy, I told you to do it that way, but the world is just twenty-four hours older, and we have advanced that much; so do it this way to-day." [10]

Boucicault's occasional asperity is an understandable limitation, for actors as a group are not in the first rank of our intellectuals.

Indeed, it has been often suggested that too much intellect handicaps an actor. Emotional perception and mimetic ability are probably a great deal more important than rational understanding to an actor. Boucicault's own chief handicap as a director would seem to be an occasional failure to realize that the understanding of his actors was not keeping pace with his own lively fancy and volatile imagination. To easily baffled actors, an ebulliently inventive director who keeps tinkering with the production is usually a greater danger than a more phlegmatic one who gets the movements and the business "fixed" at an early date. Nevertheless, in the best of all possible worlds, and sometimes even in this one, an inventive and imaginative director is infinitely preferable to an imitative, pedestrian one.

III   *On Theatrical Management*

Boucicault's influence on theatrical management was important but rather double-edged. As a manager himself, producing primarily his own plays, he was interested, like the present-day producer, in making as much money from a show as possible. He was usually quite successful as the manager of a touring company, but rather a failure as the owner or lessee of a theater. His attempts at establishing permanent theaters in New Orleans; New York; Washington, D.C.; and London all failed—and the main reason seems to have been a too grandiose planning and a too extravagant expenditure. He had magnificent conceptions, but he was a better tactician than strategist.

His main contributions to management are succinctly summed up by Walsh:

He reduced the length of dramatic entertainments, which had frequently lasted from seven o'clock till past midnight. Managers were in the habit of offering three or four pieces nightly: he gave one important drama. He abolished the practice of admitting the public for half price at nine o'clock. But the most important of all innovations, and one which wholly changed theatrical conditions both in England and America, was effected by him in 1861. Previous to this year, each prominent theatre had its own company; the "stock" system prevailed; and the great stars from London and New York, when they visited a provincial theatre, were supported by the local "stock." Boucicault contended that such stars would not prove magnets if they did not appear in the new plays in which they had been successful in the metropolis. It was the play, he affirmed, and not the star, that drew the money. He pointed out that the author of such a play received as his royalty a mere pittance—sometimes thirty shillings a night—while the star was paid more than thirty times that amount. Taking advantage of the success of "The Colleen Bawn," he engaged a company of actors. . . . He offered the *play* as the *star*, with this satellite company, to the provincial managers. They demurred till one of them consented to give the scheme a trial. The result was an unqualified success. For several years he sent out specially organized companies with his plays, thereby deriving immense revenues. Then followed the disintegration of local "stock companies," till at length few theatres maintained resident companies, but depended solely on touring organizations, which system now prevails generally.[11]

There were other contributions such as his experiments with fireproofing the stage scenery and his popularization of the matinee. But largely Boucicault's influence tended to limit the powers of the manager. As a manager, he produced primarily his own plays; but, as an author, he had many dealings with other managers, and his main influence tended to increase at the expense of the manager the rights and revenue of the author. Really, he considered himself not primarily a manager but an author, and he once caustically remarked:

As a low state of health is liable to let in a score of maladies, so a low state of the drama has developed the *commercial manager*. This person in most instances received his education in a bar-room, possibly on the far side of the counter. The more respectable may have been gamblers. Few of them could compose a bill of the play where the spelling and grammar would not disgrace an urchin under ten years of age. These men have obtained possession of first-class theatres, and assume to exercise the artistic and literary functions required to select the actors, to read and determine the merit of dramatic works, and preside generally over the highest and noblest efforts of the human mind. The great theatres of London are filled by men of this class who have thus succeeded to the curule chairs of John Philip Kemble, Richard Brinsley Sheridan, Macready, George Colman, and Charles Kean. To the commercial manager we owe the introduction of the burlesque, opera bouffe, and the reign of buffoonery. We owe him

also the deluge of French plays that set in with 1842, and
swamped the English drama of that period.[12]

Indeed, Boucicault's chief theatrical reforms sprang from the fact
that he "was an author; his object was to benefit his craft—to
obtain for the dramatist not only the place of honor at the entertainment, but the largest share of the loaves and the fishes." [13]
Very early in his career, the young author of *London Assurance*
had offered, as we have noted, the manager Ben Webster a new
play, and been told that it was no longer necessary to pay authors
£300 to £500 for an untried script, when a piece successfully
produced in Paris could be translated for only £25. This rebuff
focused the exploitation of the playwright quite clearly in Boucicault's mind. He saw that, "While managers and star actors were
reaping a golden harvest by means of the dramatic works fur-
nished by the phalanx of dramatists, the authors received a
miserable pittance of thirty dollars a week for the use of such
plays as 'Richelieu,' 'The Rent Day,' and 'London Assurance.' " [14]
His residence in France taught him that French dramatists received 10 per cent of the gross receipts, and on his return to
England he tried unsuccessfully to persuade the leading members
of the Dramatic Authors' Society to embrace this system. He had
no luck; and, "Finding himself defeated and disregarded by the
London managers," he sailed in 1853 to New York.

There he did accomplish something tangible for the author in
his work for a revision of the American copyright law. The law
of 1831 was inadequate and protected only American citizens in
America, and it did not even protect them well. The author had
to bargain individually with an actor-manager for his payment;
and, once having sold a play to an actor, the author had no right
to publish it. Indeed, publishing was foolish; for, when a play
was in print, it could easily be pirated by other producers or
other printers.

"No wonder," wrote Robert Montgomery Bird, whose experiences with the actor Edwin Forrest had turned him away from
drama to fiction, "so few American poets are willing to try their
fortunes on the stage where the risk is great and the condition
of Success is the surrendering of every aspiration for literary
fame." [15] These lines were written to the younger American
dramatist George Henry Boker, also a sufferer under the existing

copyright law. Bird advised Boker, who had drafted a Dramatic Authors' Bill, to go to Washington to enlist the feelings of a few leading members of the House in its favor. Boker pressed the matter for two or three years, but it was only when Boucicault vigorously joined him in 1855 that they succeeded in getting the bill brought before Congress, which ultimately passed it on August 18, 1856.

This law, as Boucicault wrote later, gave to "the author of a drama or the composer of a musical work, in addition to the sole right of printing and publishing, with the sole right also of representing it or permitting it to be represented." [16] The act was far from perfect; for one thing, only the title of a play was registered, rather than the entire script being deposited in the Library of Congress as is the situation now. Such registration made it difficult to prove infringements. Nevertheless, Boucicault himself was well aware of his rights; and the first arrest under the law occurred in Boston in November, 1856, when Boucicault accused the producers of *Rose; or, The Career of an Actress* of stealing his copyright piece *Violet; or, The Career of an Actress*.

Boucicault was hardly impelled by altruistic motives in his work for the copyright law. He was mainly—perhaps only—concerned in protecting his own work; and, even after the passage of the law, he had not the least hesitation in continuing his piratical raids on French dramatic literature and, indeed, any place that suggested a fertile idea. Sometimes he quite generously acknowledged his source, but I doubt that he usually paid any royalties.

About ten years later, in England, with such attractive plays to offer as *The Colleen Bawn* and *The Poor of New York*, Boucicault could and did demand a percentage of the receipts. If he had not quite liberated all dramatic authors, he had gone a very long way toward liberating himself.

IV On Playwriting

Boucicault's contemporary influence on his fellow playwrights was vast and not particularly healthy, for he fostered in his most influential works a brainless, crowd-pleasing, spectacular, and simplistic kind of entertainment. It would be possible, I think, to

devote many pages to Boucicault's influence on fortunately forgotten dramatists. It is probably more important, though, to trace
the lingering, the current influence, of Boucicault.

In our day, the specific literary influence of Boucicault has not
been widespread, but three of our century's greatest dramatists
were touched by it. Allardyce Nicoll has noted how Bernard
Shaw in the trial scene of *The Devil's Disciple* seemed to imitate
the trial scene in *Arrah-na-Pogue*.[17] Martin Meisel in *Shaw and
the Nineteenth Century Theatre* has noted how the century's
theatrical conventions and devices are so often exploited by him.
Indeed, Shaw with his usual candor has admitted that "my stage
tricks and suspenses and thrills and jests are the ones in vogue
when I was a boy, by which time my grandfather was tired of
them." [18] To take but one example, the practicable automobile
in *Man and Superman* is precisely what Boucicault would have
done had he lived long enough to see an automobile.

Many of Shaw's early plays were little more than nineteenth-
century melodramas or farces turned inside out. One would not
have to look far in the nineteenth-century drama to discover the
simple ancestors of *The Devil's Disciple, Captain Brassbound's
Conversion, Arms and the Man, The Shewing Up of Blanco
Posnet,* or *Androcles and the Lion.* This influence was not usually
directly from Boucicault, but it was Boucicault's kind of theater.
Having appreciated its excellences, Shaw could assimilate it into
his own brand of theater. Having learned from the nineteenth-
century entertainments some crucial points about theatrical necessity, Shaw was rarely in danger of writing half-dramatized
tracts.

In a list of authors that Shaw recommended to a fledgling
drama critic, the only dramatists from nineteenth-century England were Boucicault and Robertson—and Shaw included them
in a company with the Greeks, Molière, Goethe, and Ibsen.[19]
This inclusion would seem to indicate that he highly valued the
nineteenth-century theater of Boucicault, Brougham, and Daly
for the knowledge it gave him of how overwhelmingly important
the craft of entertainment is for the art of the drama.

Boucicault also seems to have been an important influence on
John Millington Synge and perhaps a crucial influence on Synge's
greatest play, *The Playboy of the Western World.* Synge did not

know Boucicault's work until 1904 when he saw *The Shaughraun*
at the Queen's Theatre, Dublin, and wrote the following pertinent
remarks:

> Some recent performances of *The Shaughraun* at the Queen's
> Theatre in Dublin have enabled local playgoers to make an in-
> teresting comparison between the methods of the early Irish
> melodrama and those of the Irish National Theatre Society. It is
> unfortunate for Dion Boucicault's fame that the absurdity of his
> plots and pathos has gradually driven people of taste away from
> his plays, so that at the present time few are perhaps aware what
> good acting comedy some of his work contains. The characters
> of Conn the Shaughraun and in a lesser degree those of Mrs
> Kelly and Moya as they were played the other day by members
> of Mr Kennedy Miller's company, had a breadth of naive humour
> that is now rare on the stage. Mr James O'Brien especially, in the
> part of Conn, put a genial richness into his voice that it would be
> useless to expect from the less guttural vocal capacity of French
> or English comedians, and in listening to him one felt how much
> the modern stage has lost in substituting impersonal wit for
> personal humour. It is fortunate for the Irish National Theatre
> Society that it has preserved—in plays like *The Pot of Broth*—a
> great deal of what was best in the traditional comedy of the Irish
> stage, and still has contrived by its care and taste to put an end
> to the reaction against the careless Irish humour of which every-
> one has had too much. The effects of this reaction, it should be
> added, are still perceptible in Dublin, and the Irish National
> Theatre Society is sometimes accused of degrading Ireland's vi-
> sion of herself by throwing a shadow of the typical Stage Irish-
> man upon her mirror.[20]

Synge and the other early dramatists of the Abbey Theatre were
writing in reaction to an absurdly farcical or sentimentally romantic view of the Irishman. Indeed, perhaps one of the most
fruitful ways of regarding Synge's *The Playboy of the Western
World* is to see it as an attempt to measure the broth-of-a-bhoy
stage Irishman by the standards of realistic comedy. And even
further, to show how Ireland seemed impelled to manufacture
this laughing boy out of even the most obdurate material. For
instance, Christy Mahon, that absurd playboy, is really a low,
mean, unprepossessing, dirty runt of a fellow who is fleeing in
holy terror from a squalid domestic quarrel.

Pegeen Mike, the Widow Quinn, and the neighborhood girls treat Christy's presumed murder of his father as a high, heroic exploit; and slowly Christy takes on all of the speciously glamorous qualities of the laughing, swaggering, devil-may-care vagabond. In the last act, in a Boucicaultian scene right out of *Flying Scud* or *The Jilt*, Christy wins the horse race; and, for a moment, he becomes a Conn the Shaughraun. Then, when it is found that he has not really killed his father, Pegeen and the others turn on him; and two interesting psychological developments occur.

First, Christy, repudiated by the society that has re-created him, becomes a true hero. He is now really free in a way that Conn, Myles, and Shaun the Post never were. He has to play no silly social role any more, for he is a free, a mentally liberated Shaughraun. At the same time, Pegeen's reaction is a revealing criticism of the Irish character. "I have killed," she laments, "the only playboy of the Western World." Basically, then, in this play Synge is criticizing the ingrained need in the Irish character for romance, for the creation of a hero—a need which Boucicault also realized and which he flattered in his best Irish entertainments.

Usually, I distrust generalizations about national characteristics, but here there seems something to it. We see this yearning for romance not only in Boucicault but also in many other Irish writers—in Carleton, in Lever, in Lover, in the patriotic melodramas of Whitbread and P. J. Bourke. We see it in politics: Parnell was the uncrowned king; the ex-mathematics instructor De Valera is said to understand the Einstein theory. We see it in Yeats and Stephens. We see it in the work of the best new Irish playwrights—in Michael J. Molloy's *The Visiting House* and in Bryan MacMahon's *The Song of the Anvil*, for instance. Boucicault knew his Ireland well, and Synge's playboy is merely Conn the Shaughraun come of age.

The third major Irish writer to be influenced by Boucicault was Sean O'Casey, and he was influenced the most deeply of all. As a young man, he had played in amateur performances of Shakespeare and Boucicault. Indeed, on the stage of the old Mechanics Theatre, which was to become in later years the Abbey of Yeats and Synge, he once played the role of Father Dolan in *The Shaughraun*. The earliest and probably the two most lasting theatrical influences on O'Casey were the seemingly incongruous pair, Shakespeare and Boucicault.

The Boucicault influence is pervasive in O'Casey's work, and we see it particularly in the blending of comedy and tragedy that was so striking in O'Casey's early plays. He himself has written:

> As for blending "Comedy with Tragedy," it's no new practice—hundreds have done it, including Shakespeare up to Dion Boucicault in, for instance "Colleen Bawn" & "Conn, the Shaughraun." And, indeed, Life is always doing it, doing it, doing it. Even where one lies dead, laughter is often heard in the next room. There's no tragedy that isn't tinged with humour, no comedy that hasn't its share of tragedy—if one has eyes to see, ears to hear. Sorrow & Joy are sisters, though Joy isn't always Joy or Sorrow Sorrow; they change appearance often & rapidly.[21]

Although Boucicault is often condemned for an unreal theatricality, O'Casey saw in this central Boucicaultian device an opportunity to give a more realistic view of life than that usually offered by the stage. After *The Plough and the Stars* of 1926, O'Casey changed his style and no longer wrote in the manner of his early masterpieces, but he never did dispense with the Boucicaultian device of juxtaposing incongruous emotions. We see it as strongly in his late plays as we do in his early ones.

Another quality that O'Casey, like Shaw, took from Boucicault was an awareness of the more sensuous theatrical qualities of the drama. Like Boucicault, O'Casey wove songs and snatches of songs throughout his work. Plays like *Red Roses for Me, The Bishop's Bonfire, Purple Dust,* and *Figuro in the Night* contain not only songs but dances. In all of the late plays, the vivid colors of the costumes and the sets are exactly described. *Within the Gates,* the second act of *The Silver Tassie,* the third act of *Red Roses,* and a great deal of *Cock-a-Doodle Dandy* depend for their effect on rather complicated visual spectacle.

O'Casey's clearest tribute to Boucicault appears in *The Drums of Father Ned* where he writes an actual pastiche of a Boucicaultian patriotic melodrama. The young people of Doonavale are planning a Tostal, and as one of its main events are rehearsing an old play. Despite the archaic staginess of the dialogue, O'Casey means this scene to be played straight rather than hoaked up.[22] He is interested in exploiting the residue of vitality in the form.

His actors are all in colorful period costume: the hero "in the garb of a gentleman leader of the Ninety-eight insurgents—dark-green tailed coat, white shirt with white-frilled stock, white knee-breeches, and polished top-boots. A light-green shoulder-sash carries a sword hanging on his left hip." His English captain is wearing a "crimson cutaway coat, the frock-flaps turned back, showing a blue lining; he wears white buckskin breeches and top-boots, and the cuffs of his red coat are blue, ornamented with gold braid; his shoulders are decorated with gold epaulettes. He wears a dark-crimson sash round his waist, and carries a sword by his left side." Indeed, Casey is only describing the costume of Major Molineux and Robert Ffolliott. He is glorying in the convention and not apologizing for it; and we can see that fact also in the stilted and stirring dialogue:

MICHAEL: We are young, and God has given us strength and courage and counsel. May He give us the victory!

TOM (*Indignantly*): This, sir, is high treason!

MICHAEL: That is our stand; that is our story; and that is our resolution. It is high time for a change, for the Republican principle that all men are equal, that they should have the right to declare who shall govern them, and that the law should be beneficial, not to the few, but to the many. Your peace, Captain, within the life we live, is but quiet decay.

TOM (*Furiously*): I arrest you, Michael Binnington, for high treason against this realm and the realm's law; I arrest you in the King's name! Hand me your sword!

MICHAEL (*Slapping his hand on the hilt of his sword*): Come and take it!

MAN (*From the back running forward and shouting*): Our chapel's on fire! The Yeomanry are settin' it ablaze!

MICHAEL (*To Man of the Musket*): Gather the men together, Pat, by the risin' of th' moon, and we shall march.

TOM (*Drawing his sword*): Defend yourself, you traitor! [23]

In sum, O'Casey took from Boucicault not only the perception about comedy and tragedy existing together, but also a high verve, a delight in flamboyant language, in color, in dance, in music, and in spectacle.

A few other Irish playwrights have been somewhat influenced by Boucicault. Denis Johnston is basically as un-Boucicaultian a writer as is possible, but he does effectively exploit the Boucicaultian patriotic melodrama as a springboard and as a major theme for his richly complex satire of modern Ireland, *The Old*

Lady Says "No!" Paul Vincent Carroll's major influences are probably Ibsen, the Catholic Church, and the Augustan Age of English literature. He has, however, one untypical play, *The Old Foolishness*, in which the character of Dan is clearly a descendant of Conn and Myles. Perhaps also the geniality of his "satirical extravaganza" *The Devil Came from Dublin* owes something also to the spirit of Boucicault, for the dashing hero and the wild harebrained heroine could easily have been written by Dion. Brinsley MacNamara, the Abbey playwright, was a Boucicault buff who spent years fruitlessly searching for a copy of Walsh's rare biography. MacNamara is a writer of at least one powerful tragedy as well as several deft, popular comedies. His play most reminiscent of Boucicault is a horse-racing drama, *The Glorious Uncertainty*, which seems fairly closely modeled on *Flying Scud*.

One of the best recent Irish playwrights is Michael J. Molloy who must surely take his place with Synge, Fitzmaurice, and O'Casey as a creator of the richest dramatic dialogue to emerge from the Irish Renaissance. Molloy is a more muted spirit than Boucicault, but his fine historical plays, such as *The King of Friday's Men* or *The Paddy Pedlar*, are stirring examples of what Boucicault might have written had he had more of a lyrical bent and less of a crowd-pleasing entertainer in his makeup. Molloy's *The Will and the Way* is a contemporary play which concerns the amateur production of a typical Irish melodrama, like *The Shaughraun, The Colleen Bawn, The Land She Loved,* or *By the Shannon's Shore*. Although *The Will and the Way* is minor Molloy, it is ripely theatrical, and much of its excellence derives from its evocation of an older kind of theater.

The most prolific and certainly one of the most talented of the new Irish dramatists is John B. Keane who has confessed his indebtedness to Molloy, and in whom may be seen a number of Boucicaultian characteristics—a frequent use of song, high spirits, verve, and an unabashed use of melodrama. The hero of his muted piece of realism *The Year of the Hiker* is actually a kind of antidote both to Synge's Playboy and to Boucicault's Shaughraun, for it shows what happens in the modern world when the Shaughraun grows old, feeble, and tired.

The closest emulator of Boucicault among the present Irish writers is Seamus de Burca, whose father P. J. Bourke managed the Queen's Theatre, the home of Irish melodrama, and wrote

several patriotic melodramas himself. De Burca has published an
edition of *Arrah-na-Pogue,* and has himself made a highly successful dramatization of Kickham's novel *Knocknagow,* in precisely the form and spirit of Boucicault.

However, this influence hunting is at best a tenuous business;
and it would be possible to go through many Irish playwrights,
from Lady Gregory to de Burca's cousins the Behan brothers,
and find Boucicault-like qualities in much of their work. How
much of this influence is specifically from Boucicault, who was
often played until quite recently in Ireland, and how much of it
is simply a part of the general Irish dramatic heritage is impossible to determine. Still, as the recent brilliant revivals of *The
Colleen Bawn* and *The Shaughraun* at the Abbey Theatre indicate, the spirit of Boucicault is not dead in the Irish theatre.

Until about 1914 or 1920, the American theater was still in its
nonage, and its high priest was still David Belasco. Belasco was
really the last significant twitch of the Boucicault tradition in
the American theater. He admired Dion, he was much influenced
by him, he had been briefly his amanuensis when Boucicault was
appearing at Piper's Opera House in Virginia City, and he had
later made a revision of *The Octoroon.* The typical Belasco play,
such as *The Girl of the Golden West,* is little more than Boucicault rewritten. An easy pathos, a nice excitement, a simplification of emotion—all of these qualities are basic to the Boucicault
formula; and they are what made Belasco, for all of his pseudo-
realism, the last twitch of the old artificial theater of entertainment.

About the only American playwright to be influenced in recent
years by Boucicault was Elmer Rice, and that influence was
totally accidental. In the late 1920's, Rice had been offering his
masterly *Street Scene* to every producer who would look at it,
and he was receiving only rejections and rebuffs. Finally, old
William A. Brady, who had managed the theatrical career of
"Gentleman Jim" Corbett and who had bought *After Dark* from
Boucicault only to become involved in a lengthy lawsuit with
Augustin Daly over the play, was struck by the resemblance of
Street Scene to Dion's *The Poor of New York.*[24] And for that
reason he accepted the piece which became the hit of the season,
won the Pulitzer Prize, and remains one of the glories of the
modern American drama. Rice himself remarked, "My acquaint-

ance with Boucicault was limited to W. S. Gilbert's allusion to him in *Patience,* so I did not know whether to feel complimented or not." [25]

Actually, in America the appearance of Rice and O'Neill in 1914 signaled the end of the nineteenth-century drama of Boucicault and Belasco. Already Zola, Ibsen, Chekhov, and Strindberg had made themselves felt upon the Continent; and Bernard Shaw and Granville Barker had established themselves in England. The old era was over, and Boucicault himself in his last years seemed to sense the fact. In an 1877 article called "The Decline of the Drama," Boucicault looked back over the last hundred years of the drama and remarked that in that time

> . . . the mind of mankind has been eagerly devoted to the application of scientific discoveries to useful purposes, and particularly to the unification of political and commercial interests. Information has become a drug; investigation has set bounds to romance and rendered fancy ridiculous. The whole world is plotted out and turned into real estate. The island of Prospero is a thriving settlement, and if Rosalind should trespass into the forest of Ardennes, a sturdy keeper would take her into custody.[26]

The Shakespeare of this world "is occupied in editing a morning newspaper," [27] and the Michelangelo "is inventing a sewing-machine." It was an age, he thought, that required the dramatist to be practical: "He must not consider anything too deeply; his audience cannot follow him. He must not soar; their prosaic minds, heavy with facts, cannot rise. He cannot roam; their exact information turns him back at every step. I earnestly believe the human mind always maintains the same average level. There is always a Homer, a Virgil, a Dante, and a Shakespeare in existence, but mankind is pleased not to call them forth." [28] He then concluded the article, which was addressed to Charles Reade, by sadly remarking: "When our people shall demand the highest class of dramatic entertainment, a Shakespeare and a Garrick will appear. Until then, my dear friend, the world will rest contented with such poor things as you and me." [29]

Boucicault's last remarks on the drama appeared shortly after his death in an article called "The Future American Drama." Not everything that Boucicault prophesied in that article was accurate, but he did make some palpable hits. He realized that the old drama had had its day on the stage, and he recognized something of the vitality of the new drama of Europe that was being exemplified in the plays of Ibsen and Zola. He did not entirely like Naturalism in the theater and described it as "a philosophical school of sociology, for the illustration and argument of ethical problems" [30]—a description that would have well satisfied Bernard Shaw. Boucicault thought that a new drama was evolving in America which would be "prosaic and positive," which would reflect the period, and which would emphasize character more than an arrangement of startling incidents. He was right, but that drama was still twenty-five or thirty years away.

V *Curtain*

The spirit of Boucicault lived on into the twentieth century, but it was not so apparent on the stage as it was in the films, and then in radio, and now on television. He would have been quite at home in those mediums, for modern popular entertainment has been little more than Boucicault rewritten—and usually not written as well. I am suggesting no direct influence of Boucicault on D. W. Griffith or Cecil B. De Mille, but popular entertainment continues to tap the same emotions and to use even the same devices and the identical situations that we find in nineteenth-century melodramas. It is no compliment to humanity to note its continuing desire for thrills and tears, but man has changed little in the last hundred years, and Boucicault would feel as at home with the television audience of today as he did with the theater audience of yesterday. Yesterday's *Jezebel* is only today's *Peyton Place,* and it will be many tomorrows and tomorrows before Shavian He-Ancients and She-Ancients feel no compulsion to quiver and cry at swashbucklers and tear-jerkers.

What finally remains from all of this mass of work that can take an honorable place in dramatic literature? Not a great deal, but certainly the Regency comedies and farces of Boucicault's youth may make a strong bid. The best of the comedies, *Old Heads and Young Hearts* and *London Assurance,* do not rank with the great English comedies. *London Assurance* is a bit too brittle, and *Old Heads* is a bit too hard. But somewhere—not too far behind Sheridan, Goldsmith, and Farquhar—these plays may take up an honorable position in the enduring minor drama, along with the plays of Etherege, Cibber, Aphra Behn, and Colman the Elder. And that really is no ignoble position at all. But perhaps, to make my judgment more pertinent, I should make a rather artificial comparison. Boucicault's Regency comedies do not seem to me quite so full-bodied as the modern comedies of Somerset Maugham, but they seem considerably more substantial than the modern comedies of such successful recent playwrights as Philip Barry, S. N. Behrman, Terence Rattigan, or John Van Druten. Boucicault's Regency farces must pale—as what farces must not?—in comparison with Oscar Wilde's *The Importance of Being Earnest* or even Bernard Shaw's *Arms and the Man,* but they seem quite sturdy when compared to a flimsy bit of fluff like Noel Coward's *Private Lives.*

The drama lost an excellent comic writer when Boucicault became wedded to the commercial stage. He had a beautiful eye for absurdity, and Ben Jonson himself would have admitted the effectiveness of some of the "humours" in these early plays, just as Synge did admit the effectiveness of the "humor" of the later ones. Boucicault had an adroit way with a complicated plot of comic intrigue. Above all, he had a superb facility in writing banter, repartee, and good-humored badinage. Had he been able to continue writing in the strain in which he began, English dramatic literature of the late nineteenth century might have been inestimably richer.

Instead, he was deflected into the commercial theater, and poured out his great mass of crowd-pleasing entertainments. Here and there, plays like *The Knight of Arva, The Octoroon,* and *The Jilt* show many traces of his old comic talent. But, more often than not, this excellent comedy was watered down by a platitudinous theme, a cloying dose of sentiment, or stiltedly stereotyped characterization. Too often the comedy was but a momentary relief from some spectacular excitement or breathtaking twist of plot.

The bulk of this commercial work—and, indeed, the bulk of Boucicault—is mere entertainment, too simple to reflect reality and too trivial to engage our deepest interest. Some of this entertainment was extremely successful in its day, and if *The Phantom* or *Belle Lamar* were revived today they might still have a twitch or two of stage life about them. A fairly recent off-Broadway revival of *The Poor of New York* showed that the play was still good theatrical hokum—which, of course, was all that it ever was. Nevertheless, most of these commercial entertainments, the good ones and the bad ones, are dead and forgotten; and their yellowing pages are gathering dust on the bottom shelves of libraries. And that probably is a good thing, for we will never have a shortage of trivial entertainment.

Boucicault is most remembered today for his three best Irish plays—*The Colleen Bawn, Arrah-na-Pogue,* and *The Shaughraun.* To my mind, these plays do not have quite the literary merit of the Regency comedies, however. The Irish plays are theatrically excellent—indeed, they are almost theatrically foolproof. And they do contain, in addition to their plentiful humor and excitement, a tincture of real feeling that was often lacking in Boucicault's work. It is, however, a tincture, a hint, a somewhat spurious reminiscence of pure feeling rather than the real thing. The more or less straight characters in the plays are definitely better and fuller than the straight characters of popular melodrama, but they are still only caricature of reality, and their emotions are only simplifications of real emotions.

Also, although Boucicault doubtless felt for his country, he studiously avoided a real clash of issues in these plays. As in *The Octoroon,* where there was nothing to offend either the North or the South, so in these Irish plays there is nothing to offend either the English or the Irish. Both sides are given their due so thoroughly that the Irish problem seems to have been an inexplicable and not very important historical accident for which no one was responsible, and which doubtless would be wafted entirely away in the aura of good feeling surrounding the concluding marriages and happy endings. This genial ignoring of the problem is considerably more salutary than the cant patriotism of *Robert Emmet;* nevertheless, its general effect is to take the plays out of reality and to place them in a nostalgic, romanticized, postcard version of Ireland.

Probably our ultimate feelings about Boucicault are a bit contradictory. There is an enthusiastic, not wholly critical delight that we can take even in some of his balder works—a delight in craftsmanship, in color, in song, in unbridled emotionalism, in theatrical magic. But there is also a nagging regret that so excellent and facile and prolific a talent should have been so debased by the nineteenth-century commercial theater. Still, that is the way of the world of the theater; and there are only a few Shaws and O'Caseys who can indomitably hold out against it. To have been a Shaw or an O'Casey would have been a triumph, but any one could feel quite complacent about having been only a Cibber, a Garrick, a Colman, a Robertson, a Maugham—or a Dion Boucicault!

Notes and References

Preface

1. J. M. Synge, Preface to *The Tinker's Wedding*, in *The Complete Works of John M. Synge* (New York, 1935), p. 177.

Chapter One

1. Julius H. Tolson in his "Dion Boucicault" (Unpublished doctoral dissertation, University of Pennsylvania, 1951) remarks on p. 9 that Anne Darley married Boursiquot in 1813, and cites in substantiation the *Appendix to Thirtieth Report of the Deputy Keeper of The Public Records in Ireland* (Dublin, 1899). However, Albert E. Johnson in his article "The Birth of Dion Boucicault," *Modern Drama*, XI (September, 1968) remarks on p. 157 that Anna Maria Darley and Boursiquot were married at the Protestant St. Thomas's Church in Dublin on July 29, 1813, and states that a copy of the marriage certificate is in his possession.

2. According to Boucicault, neither uncle gave him much literary encouragement: ". . . . both George and Charles Darley had regarded his efforts as those of a runaway schoolboy, who deserved to be whipped back to his lessons." From "Early Days of a Dramatist," *North American Review*, CXLVIII (May, 1889), p. 589.

3. H. Hale Bellot, *University College, London: 1826–1926* (London, 1929), pp. 131 and 133.

4. Townsend Walsh, *The Career of Dion Boucicault* (New York, 1915), pp. 7–8.

5. Calthrop's information is contained in Johnson's "The Birth of Dion Boucicault," pp. 159–60.

6. Quoted in Tolson, p. 4.

7. In particular, note Boucicault's article "The Debut of a Dramatist," *North American Review*, CXLVIII (April, 1889), in which the assertion about his birth is repeated several times.

8. Quoted in Johnson, p. 158.

9. *Ibid.*, p. 162.

10. Frank Dalton, "Small-Change and Boucicault," *The Dublin Magazine*, I (November, 1923), p. 283. Micheal O hAodha, in his

article "The Quest for Boucicault," *Plays and Places* (Dublin, 1961) repeats the assertion about Dr. Geoghegan's Academy.

11. From an autobiographical article in the New York *World*, May 15, 1887, quoted in Walsh, p. 11.

12. Information in an article by Agnes Robertson clipped from an unidentified newspaper, and also from a letter to the present writer by Christopher Calthrop, October 4, 1965.

13. John Coleman, *Charles Reade, As I Knew Him* (London, 1903), p. 13. Coleman also remarks, "I can well believe what Charles Mathews, Walter Lacey, and John Brougham often told me—that in his *juvenilia* he was the most fascinating young scapegrace that ever baffled or bamboozled a bailiff." P. 14.

14. From the New York *World*, May 15, 1887. Quoted in Walsh, p. 14.

15. Walsh, p. 16.

16. According to Boucicault's friend John Brougham, the well-known actor and playwright, "Boucicault's voice sounds like the rattling of broken china at the bottom of a dry well." Quoted in William Winter, *Other Days* (New York, 1908), p. 111.

17. *The Brighton Dramatic Miscellany*, July 31, 1838. Quoted in Tolson, p. 15.

18. Coleman, p. 16.

19. From an unidentified clipping of a newspaper article, "Her Life with Boucicault," quoted in Tolson, p. 26.

20. Boucicault, "The Debut of a Dramatist," p. 454.

21. George Rowell, *The Victorian Theatre, A Survey* (London, 1956), p. 1.

22. Boucicault, "Early Days of a Dramatist," p. 592.

23. *Ibid.*

24. Boucicault, "The Decline of the Drama," *North American Review*, CXXV (September, 1877), p. 243.

25. Clement Scott, *The Drama of Yesterday and Today* (London, 1899), Vol. I, p. 105.

26. Tolson, pp. 109–10.

27. Quoted in Walsh, pp. 58–59.

28. Walsh, pp. 155–56.

29. Coleman, p. 277.

30. Walsh, p. 120.

31. *Ibid.*, pp. 126–27.

32. Tolson, p. 257.

Chapter Two

1. Indeed, Boucicault in his last published article remarked: "Originality in drama does not mean the invention of new subjects, new

intrigue or incidents: so little have these to do with dramatic merit that Horace advises the young dramatist to avoid new subjects and prefer such as may be familiar to the spectators, treating these in a new manner. For the important object of the dramatist is the exhibition of human character 'to which fundamental law' says Macaulay, 'every other regulation is subordinate.' " "The Future American Drama," *The Arena*, II (November, 1890), p. 643.

Chapter Three

1. Dalton, p. 284.
2. Quoted in Dion Boucicault, *Forbidden Fruit & Other Plays*, eds. Allardyce Nicoll and F. Theodore Cloak (Princeton, 1940), p. 110.
3. Arthur Hobson Quinn, ed., *Representative American Plays, From 1767 to the Present Day* (New York, 1953), p. 402.
4. Walsh, p. 108.
5. Quoted in Walsh, pp. 109–10. Boucicault has another similar account in "Leaves from a Dramatist's Diary," *North American Review*, CXLIX (August, 1889), pp. 233–34.
6. Quoted in *The Dolmen Boucicault*, ed. David Krause (Dublin, 1964), p. 25.
7. A. Nicholas Vardac, *Stage to Screen: Theatrical Method from Garrick to Griffith* (Cambridge, Mass., 1949).
8. Rowell, p. 57.
9. Boucicault, "Leaves from a Dramatist's Diary," p. 234.

Chapter Four

1. Squire and Marie Bancroft, *The Recollections of Sixty Years* (London, 1909), p. 195.
2. Quoted in Sean McMahon's "The Wearing of the Green: The Irish Plays of Dion Boucicault," *Eire–Ireland*, II (Summer, 1957), p. 110.
3. Micheál MacLiammóir, the brilliant Irish actor, in his one-man show *I Must Be Speaking to my Friends*, sometimes uses this section of *Arrah-na-Pogue* as an example of flagrant stage-Irishness. Droll as his attack is, he recites the lines with a broadness that unfairly exaggerates a certain tradition. If the scene were done with an underplayed naturalness, it would be, I believe, as charming and convincing as those comic scenes in *The Shaughraun*, which so impressed the English critics when the Abbey Theatre took the play to the World Theatre Festival in London in the summer of 1968.
4. A close look at Tom Broadbent's scenes with Nora Reilly in *John Bull's Other Island* shows some moderate similarities to Molineux' scenes with Claire.

5. From the Boston *Journal* of Feburary 21, 1888. Quoted in Tolson, p. 290.

Chapter Five

1. In *A Memoir of Edward Askew Sothern* (London, 1890), Pemberton also remarks on page 30: "Mr. E. H. Sothern still possesses, and it need hardly be said, prizes, the long frock-coat which, on the occasion of the first performance of 'Our American Cousin' in America, his father borrowed from Mr. Boucicault for the use of *Lord Dundreary*. The name of 'Boucicault' is affixed to this, the original of a since world-famous garment."

2. Boucicault, "Coquelin—Irving," *North American Review*, CXLV (August, 1887), p. 158.

3. *Ibid.*

4. Boucicault, "My Pupils," *North American Review*, CXLVII (October, 1888), p. 436.

5. *Ibid.*, p. 437.

6. *Ibid.*, p. 436.

7. Sydney Dark and Rowland Grey, *W. S. Gilbert* (London, 1923), p. 59.

8. Rowell, p. 80.

9. Bancroft, p. 37.

10. Kate Ryan, *Old Boston Museum Days* (Boston, 1916), pp. 184–85.

11. Walsh, pp. 178–79.

12. Boucicault, "The Decline of the Drama," p. 243.

13. Boucicault, "Leaves from a Dramatist's Diary," p. 233.

14. *Ibid.*, p. 228.

15. Edward Sculley Bradley, *George Henry Boker, Poet and Patriot* (Philadelphia, 1927), p. 121. For Bird's difficulties with Forrest, see Curtis Dahl, *Robert Montgomery Bird* (New York, 1963), pp. 70–71.

16. Boucicault, "Leaves from a Dramatist's Diary," p. 230.

17. Allardyce Nicoll, *A History of English Drama, 1660–1900* (Cambridge, England, 1959), Vol. V, 90–91.

18. Bernard Shaw, *Complete Plays with Prefaces* (New York, 1963), Vol. III, p. lxi.

19. Bernard Shaw, *Collected Letters, 1874–1897*, ed. Dan H. Laurence (New York, 1965), p. 570.

20. From *The Academy and Literature*, June 11, 1904. Quoted in David Krause, *Sean O'Casey, The Man and His Work* (London, 1960), p. 60.

21. From *The Randolph-Macon Bulletin*, 1954. Quoted in Robert Hogan, *The Experiments of Sean O'Casey* (New York, 1960), pp. 177–78.

22. Information from a conversation with O'Casey and from my own experience in directing the play.

23. Sean O'Casey, *The Drums of Father Ned* (New York, 1960), pp. 35–36.

24. There is a fascinating account of Brady's haggling with Boucicault and of his subsequent legal difficulties with Daly in Brady's memoirs, *Showman* (New York, 1937), pp. 67–72.

25. Elmer Rice, *Minority Report: An Autobiography* (New York, 1963), p. 246.

26. Boucicault, "The Decline of the Drama," p. 239.

27. One of Boucicault's *bêtes noires* was the daily newspaper, and few things incensed him more than the newspaper's drama criticism. He devoted several articles and parts of articles to flaying the press. See particularly "The Decline of the Drama," "The Decline and Fall of the Press," "At the Goethe Society," and "The Future American Drama."

28. Boucicault, "The Decline of the Drama," p. 239.

29. *Ibid.*, p. 245.

30. Boucicault, "The Future American Drama," p. 643.

Selected Bibliography

The purpose of this bibliography is to list all of the known plays of Boucicault, to list the dates of their first production, to list his articles and non-dramatic books, and to list a selected number of books and articles about him. Undoubtedly the list of plays contains some errors and omissions, but it is as correct and full as I could make it; and I believe that it is more correct and full than any other previous list. In the case of Boucicault's translations and adaptations, I have cited the original source only when the identification was irrefutable. Many of his plays were undoubtedly inspired in whole or in part by some other writer's work, but unless that inspiration was demonstrable or major I have allowed them to stand without speculation on their source.

PRIMARY SOURCES

I. Plays

A Legend of the Devil's Dyke. London: Dick's Standard Plays, No. 1043, [1898]. Produced at the Brighton Theatre, Brighton, on October 1, 1838.

Lodgings to Let. Unpublished. Produced at the Haymarket, London, on March 9, 1839.

Jack Sheppard. Unpublished. Produced at Hull, on December 28, 1839. Probably based on a novel by Harrison Ainsworth.

London Assurance. London: Printed for the Author, 1841. Produced at Covent Garden, London, on March 4, 1841.

The Irish Heiress (also called *West End*). London: Andrews, 1842. Produced at Covent Garden, London, on February 7, 1842.

A Lover by Proxy. London: Acting National Drama, Vol. 9, [1845?]. Produced at the Haymarket, London, on April 21, 1842.

Alma Mater; or, A Cure for Coquettes. London: Webster, [1842?]. Produced at the Haymarket, London, on September 19, 1842.

Curiosities of Literature. London: Webster, [1842?]. Produced at the Haymarket, London, on September 24, 1842.

The Old Guard (a revision of his first play, *Napoleon's Old Guard*). London: Dick's Standard Plays, No. 1056, [1900?]. Produced at the Princess Theatre, London, on October 9, 1842.

The Bastille. Unpublished. Produced at the Haymarket, London, on December 19, 1842.

Woman. Unpublished. Produced at the Haymarket, London, on October 2, 1843.

Victor and Hortense; or, False Pride (later revised as *Paul Lafarge; or Self-Made*). Unpublished. Produced at the Haymarket, London, on November 1, 1843.

Laying a Ghost. Unpublished. Produced at the Haymarket, London, on November 15, 1843.

Sharp's the Word. Unpublished. Produced possibly at Covent Garden, London, sometime in 1843.

Used Up. London: Acting National Drama, Vol. 15, [1848?]. Produced at the Haymarket, London, on Feburary 6, 1844. A collaboration with Charles Mathews, based on *L'Homme Blasé* of Felix-Auguste Duvert and A. T. de Lauzanne de Vauxroussel.

Lolah; or, The Wreck Light. Unpublished. Produced at the Haymarket, London, on March 25, 1844.

Love in a Sack. Unpublished. Produced at the Haymarket, London, on April 22, 1844.

Mother and Son. Unpublished. Produced at the Adelphi, London, on April 22, 1844.

Don Caesar de Bazan; or Love and Honour. London: Acting National Drama, [1844]. Produced at the Adelphi, London, on October 14, 1844. A collaboration with Ben Webster, based on the French play of the same title by P-F. Dumanoir and Adolph Dennery.

The Fox and the Goose; or, The Widow's Husband. London: Acting National Drama, [1844]. Produced at the Adelphi, London, on October 22, 1844. One-act operetta written with Ben Webster and with music by Ambroise Thomas.

Old Heads and Young Hearts. New York: French's Standard Drama, No. LXII, n.d. Produced at the Haymarket, London, on November 18, 1844.

A Soldier of Fortune; or, The Irish Settler. Unpublished. Produced at the Adelphi, London, on February 6, 1845. A collaboration with Ben Webster.

Enquire Within. Unpublished. Produced at the Lyceum, London, on August 25, 1845.

The Old School. Unpublished. Produced at the Haymarket, London, on February 5, 1846.

Who Did It; or, What's in the Wind (also called *Felo de Se—Up the Flue; or, What's in the Wind*). Unpublished. Produced at the Adelphi, London, on May 11, 1846. A collaboration with Charles Kenney.

Mr. Peter Piper; or, Found Out at Last. Unpublished. Produced at the Haymarket, London, on May 16, 1846.

The Wonderful Water Cure. London: Acting National Drama, n.d. Produced at the Haymarket, London, on July 15, 1846. A collaboration with Ben Webster.

Shakespeare in London. Unpublished. Performed somewhere in London in 1846.

The School for Scheming (later revised and retitled *Love and Money*). London: Acting National Drama, Vol. 13, [1847?]. Produced at the Haymarket, London, on February 4, 1847.

La Salamandrine. Unpublished. Produced at Covent Garden, London, on May 18, 1847. A ballet probably by Boucicault.

A Confidence. Unpublished. Produced at the Haymarket, London, on May 2, 1848.

The Knight of Arva. New York: French's Standard Drama, No. 231, [1868?]. Produced at the Haymarket, London, on November 22, 1848.

The Willow Copse. Boston: William V. Spencer, [1856?]. Produced at the Adelphi, London, on November 26, 1849. A collaboration with Charles Kenney, based on *La Closerie des Genêts* by Frederic Soulie.

La Garde Nationale (also called *The Garde Mobile*). Unpublished. Produced at the Queen's, London, on January 9, 1850.

Giralda; or, The Invisible Husband (later revised as *A Dark Night's Work*). Unpublished. Produced at the Olympic, London, on September 12, 1850. Adapted from Scribe's opera *Giralda; ou, la Nouvelle Psyche.*

A Radical Cure. Unpublished. Produced in London sometime in 1850.

A Romance in the Life of Sixtus the Fifth, entitled the Broken Vow (later called *The Pope of Rome,* and often referred to merely as *Sixtus the Fifth*). London: Hailes Lacy, 1851. Produced at the Olympic, London, on February 17, 1851. An adaptation with John Bridgeman of *L'Abbaye de Castro* by Dinaux and Lemoine.

Love in a Maze. London: Hailes Lacy, 1851. Produced at the Princess, London, on March 6, 1851.

The Queen of Spades; or, The Gambler's Secret (also called *The Dame of Spades*). London: Hailes Lacy, 1851. Produced at Drury Lane, London, on March 29, 1851. An adaptation of Scribe's *La Dame de Pique.*

O'Flannigan and the Fairies. Unpublished. Produced at the Adelphi, London, on April 21, 1851. A possible adaptation by Boucicault of a Tyrone Power play.

The Corsican Brothers; or, The Vendetta. London: Hailes Lacy,

[1852]. Produced at the Princess, London, on February 23, 1852. An adaptation of *Les Frères Corses* by Grangé and Montépin, which was in turn based on a story by Dumas père.

The Vampire (later shortened and retitled *The Phantom*). London: French, [1852?]; New York: French's Standard Drama, No. 165, 1856. Produced at the Princess, London, on June 14, 1852. An adaptation of *Le Vampire* by Carmouche, de Jouffrey, and Charles Nodier.

The Prima Donna. London: Lacy's Acting Edition, Vol. 8, [1852?]. Produced at the Princess, London, on September 18, 1852.

The Sentinel. Unpublished. Produced at the Strand, London, on January 10, 1853.

Genevieve; or, The Reign of Terror. Unpublished. Produced at the Adelphi, London, on June 20, 1853. An adaptation of *Le Chevalier de la Maison-Rouge* by Dumas and Auguste Maquet.

The Young Actress. Unpublished. Produced at Burton's, New York, on October 22, 1853. A revision of *The Manager's Daughter* by Edward Lancaster.

The Fox Hunt; or, Don Quixote the Second (later revised as *The Fox Chase*). Unpublished. Produced at Burton's, New York, on November 23, 1853.

Andy Blake; or, The Irish Diamond (later called *The Dublin Boy* and *The Irish Boy*). London: Dicks' Standard Plays, No. 556, [1884]. Produced at the Boston Museum, Boston, on March 1, 1854. An adaptation of *Le Gamin de Paris* by Bayard and Vanderburch.

Faust and Marguerite. London: French, [1854?]. Produced at the Princess, London, on April 19, 1854. An adaptation of Michel Carré's *Faust et Marguerite,* possibly not by Boucicault but by T. W. Robertson.

The Devil's In It. Unpublished. Produced at the Chestnut Street Theatre, Philadelphia, on April 21, 1854. An adaptation of Scribe's *Le Part du Diable.*

Janet Pride. Unpublished. Produced at the Metropolitan Theatre, Buffalo, on August 11, 1854.

The Fairy Star. Unpublished. Produced at the Broadway Theatre, New York, on November 6, 1854.

Apollo in New York. Unpublished. Produced at the Walnut Street Theatre, Philadelphia, on November 27, 1854.

Pierre the Foundling. Unpublished. Produced at the Adelphi, London, on December 11, 1854. An adaptation of Mme Dudevant's *François le Champ.*

Eugénie; or, A Sister's Vow. Unpublished. Produced at Drury Lane, London, on January 1, 1855.

Louis XI, in Forbidden Fruit and Other Plays. Ed. Allardyce Nicoll and F. Theodore Cloak. Princeton: Princeton University Press, 1940. Produced at the Princess, London, on January 13, 1855. An adaptation of Casimir Delavigne's play of the same name.

Agnes Robertson at Home. Unpublished. Produced at the Pelican, New Orleans, on January 23, 1855.

There's Nothing In It. Unpublished. Produced at the Walnut Street Theatre, Philadelphia, on June 29, 1855.

Grimaldi; or, Scenes in the Life of an Actress (also called *The Life of an Actress* and *Violet; or, Scenes in the Life of an Actress*). New York, 1856. Produced at the National Theatre, Cincinnati, on September 24, 1855. An adaptation of *La Vie d'une Comediènne* by Anicet-Bourgois and Théodore Barrière.

The Cat Changed into a Woman. Unpublished. Produced at the National Theatre, Washington, D.C., on October 26, 1855. Loosely adapted from Scribe's *La Chatte Metamorphosée en Femme.*

Rachel Is Coming. Unpublished. Produced at the St. Louis Theatre, St. Louis, on November 8, 1855.

The Chameleon. Unpublished. Produced at the Gaiety, New Orleans, on December 20, 1855.

Azael; or, The Prodigal. Unpublished. Produced at the Gaiety, New Orleans, on January 19, 1856. An adaptation of Scribe's *L'Enfant Prodigue.*

Una. Unpublished. Produced at the Gaiety, New Orleans, on February 10, 1856.

Blue Belle. Unpublished. Produced at Burton's, New York, on November 27, 1856. An adaptation of *Le Diable a Quatre* by Adolphe de Leuven, Mazilier, and Adolphe Adam.

George Darville. Unpublished. Produced at the Adelphi, London, on June 3, 1857.

Wanted a Widow, with Immediate Possession. New York: Samuel French, [?]. Produced at Wallack's, New York, on November 9, 1857. An adaptation made with Charles Seymour of *Monsieur Jovial, ou l'huissier chonsonnier* by Théaulon and Choquart.

The Poor of New York (also called *The Streets of New York, The Poor of Liverpool, The Streets of London, The Poor of the London Streets, The Streets of Philadelphia, The Streets of Dublin,* and *The Money Panic of '57*). New York: Samuel French, [1857?]. Produced at Wallack's, New York, on December 8, 1857. An adaptation mainly by Boucicault of *Les Pauvres de Paris* by Brisebarre and Nus.

Jessie Brown; or, The Relief of Lucknow. New York: Samuel French, 1858. Produced at Wallack's, New York, on February 22, 1858.

Pauvrette (also called *The Snow Flower*). New York: Samuel French, No. 229 of French's Standard Drama, [1858?]. Produced at Niblo's

Garden, New York, on October 4, 1858. An adaptation of *La Bergère des Alpes* by Desnoyer and Dennery.

Dot, in *Forbidden Fruit and Other Plays*. Princeton: Princeton University Press, 1940. Produced at the Winter Garden, New York, on September 14, 1859. An adaptation of Dickens' *The Cricket on the Hearth*.

Chamooni III. Unpublished. Produced at the Winter Garden, New York, on October 19, 1859. An adaptation of Scribe's *L'Hours et le Pacha*.

Smike; or, Scenes from Nicholas Nickleby. Unpublished. Produced at the Winter Garden, New York, on November 1, 1859. An adaptation of Dickens' novel.

The Octoroon; or, Life in Louisiana. New York: Printed, not published, [1851?]; also in *Representative American Plays, from 1767 to the Present Day*. Ed. Arthur Hobson Quinn. 7th Ed. New York: Appleton-Century-Crofts, 1953. Produced at the Winter Garden, New York, on December 6, 1859. A loose adaptation of Captain Mayne Reid's novel *The Quadroon*.

Jeanie Deans; or, The Heart of Mid-Lothian (also known as *The Trial of Effie Deans*). Unpublished. Produced at Keene's, New York, on January 9, 1860. An adaptation of Scott's novel *The Heart of Mid-Lothian*.

Vanity Fair. Unpublished. Produced at Keene's, New York, on March 12, 1860. Not an adaptation of Thackeray's novel.

The Colleen Bawn; or, The Brides of Garryowen. [New York]: Printed but not published, [1860?]; also in *Nineteenth Century Plays*. Ed. George Rowell. London: Oxford University Press, 1953; and in *The Dolmen Press Boucicault*. Ed. David Krause. Dublin: The Dolmen Press, 1964. Produced at Keene's, New York, on March 29, 1860. A free adaptation of Gerald Griffin's novel *The Collegians*.

The Lily of Killarney. Philadelphia, 1867. Produced at Covent Garden, London, on February 2, 1862. An operetta based on *The Colleen Bawn*, with words by Boucicault and John Oxenford, and music by Sir Jules Benedict.

Ladybird; or, Harlequin Dundreary. Unpublished. Produced at the Theatre Royal, London, on December 26, 1862.

How She Loves Him. London: Chapman & Hall, [1868]. Produced at the Prince of Wales's Theatre, Liverpool, on December 7, 1863.

Omoo; or, The Sea of Ice. Unpublished. Produced at the Royal Amphitheatre, Liverpool, on October 24, 1864. An adaptation of *La Prière des Naufragés* by Dennery and Dugue.

Arrah-na-Pogue; or, The Wicklow Wedding. London: French's Acting Edition, [1865]; also Dublin: P. J. Bourke, n.d., and in *The Dol-*

men Press Boucicault. Produced at the Old Theatre Royal, Dublin, on November 7, 1864; revised version produced at the Princess, London, on March 22, 1865.

Rip Van Winkle, in *Representative American Plays*. Produced at the Adelphi, London, on September 4, 1865. An adaptation of an earlier dramatization of Washington Irving's story.

The Parish Clerk. Unpublished. Produced at the Theatre Royal, Manchester, on July 30, 1866.

The Two Lives of Mary Leigh (also known as *Hunted Down*). Unpublished. Produced at the Prince's Theatre, Manchester, on July 30, 1866.

The Long Strike (also known as *The Strike*). New York: Samuel French, [1870?]; a printed prompt copy with annotations in Boucicault's hand, probably dating from 1866, is in the National Library of Ireland. Produced at the Lyceum, London, on September 15, 1866.

Flying Scud; or, A Four Legged Fortune, in *Favorite American Plays of the Nineteenth Century*. Ed. Barrett H. Clark. Princeton: Princeton University Press, 1943. Produced at the Holborn, London, on October 6, 1866.

Wild Goose. Unpublished. Produced at the Haymarket, London, on April 29, 1867. A revision of Lester Wallack's *Rosedale; or, The Rifle Ball*.

Foul Play. Chicago: Dramatic Publishing Co., n.d. Produced at the Holborn, London, on May 28, 1868. Boucicault's dramatization of his and Charles Reade's novel.

After Dark: A Tale of London Life. New York: De Witt's Acting Plays, No. 364, n.d. Produced at the Princess, London, on August 12, 1868.

Seraphine; or, A Devotee. Unpublished. Produced at the Queen's, London, on May 1, 1869. An adaptation of Sardou's *Séraphine*.

Presumptive Evidence (also called *Mercy Dodd*), in *Forbidden Fruit and Other Plays*. Produced at the Princess, London, on May 10, 1869. An adaptation of *Le Courrier de Lyon* by Moreau, Siraudin, and Delacour.

Formosa ("The Most Beautiful"); or, The Railroad to Ruin. [Chicago?: Dramatic Publishing Co.?], n.d. Produced at Drury Lane, London, on June 23, 1869.

Dreams. Unpublished. Produced at the Fifth Avenue Theatre, New York, on September 6, 1869. A revision of T. W. Robertson's play.

Lost at Sea; or, A London Story. Unpublished. Produced at the Adelphi, London, on October 2, 1869. A collaboration with H. J. Byron.

The Mad Boy. Unpublished. Produced at the Academy of Music, New York, on April 28, 1870. Possibly by Boucicault.

The Rapparee; or, The Treaty of Limerick. Chicago: Dramatic Publishing Co., n.d. Produced at the Princess, London, either on September 2 or 7, 1870.

Jezebel; or, The Dead Reckoning Chicago: Dramatic Publishing Co., n.d. Produced at the Holborn, London, either on December 5 or 7, 1870. An adaptation of *Le Pendu* by Anicet-Bourgeois and Michel Masson.

A Christmas Story. Unpublished. Produced at the Gaiety, London, on December 24, 1870.

Elfie; or, The Cherry Tree Inn. Chicago: Dramatic Publishing Co., n.d. Produced at the Theatre Royal, Glasgow, on March 10, 1871.

Night and Morning (also called *Kerry; or, Night and Morning*). Chicago: Dramatic Publishing Co., n.d. Produced at the Gaiety, London, on November 29, 1871. An adaptation of *La Joie Fait Peur* by Emile de Girardin.

John Bull; or, The Englishman's Fireside. Unpublished. Produced at the Gaiety, London, on July 8, 1872. A revision of George Colman's play.

Babil and Bijou; or, The Lost Regalia. Unpublished. Produced at Covent Garden, London, on August 29, 1872. A collaboration with J. R. Planché.

Daddy O'Dowd; or, Turn About Is Fair Play (later revised as *The O'Dowd; or, Life in Galway,* and still later revised as *Suil-a-mor; or, Life in Galway*). London and New York: French's Acting Editions, Vol. 156, [1909]. Produced at Booth's, New York, on March 17, 1873. An adaptation of *Les Crochets du Père Martin* by Cormon and Grangé.

Mora; or, The Golden Fetters. Unpublished. Produced at Wallack's, New York, on June 3, 1873.

Mimi. Unpublished. Produced at Wallack's, New York, on July 1, 1873. An adaptation of *La Vie de Bohème* by Théodore Barrière and Henry Murger.

Led Astray. New York and London: French, [1873?]. Produced at the Union Square Theatre, New York, on December 6, 1873. An adaptation of Octave Feuillet's *La Tentation.*

A Man of Honor. Unpublished. Produced at Wallack's, New York, on December 22, 1873. An adaptation of *Le Fils naturel* by Dumas fils.

A Struggle for Life. Unpublished and perhaps unproduced, but copyrighted by Boucicault in 1873.

Boucicault in California. Unpublished. Produced at the San Francisco Theatre, San Francisco, on January 19, 1874.

Belle Lamar (later revised as *Fin Mac Cool of Skibbereen* and also known as *Fin Maccoul*), in *Plays for the College Theatre.* Ed.

Garrett H. Leverton. New York: French, 1932. Produced at Booth's, New York, on August 10, 1874.

Venice Preserved. Unpublished. Produced at Booth's, New York, on September 14, 1874. A revision of Thomas Otway's play.

The Shaughraun. Published in acting editions by French, Dicks, Lacy's, Webster, and currently available in *The Dolmen Press Boucicault.* Produced at Wallack's, New York, on November 14, 1874.

Drink. A lost play copyrighted by Boucicault in 1874.

Free Cuba. A lost play copyrighted by Boucicault and J. J. O'Kelly in 1874.

Rafael. Unpublished. Produced at Wallack's, New York, on April 10, 1875. An adaptation of *Les Filles des Marbres* by Théodore Barrière and Lambert Thiboust, probably by Boucicault.

Forbidden Fruit. Princeton: Princeton University Press, 1940. Produced at Wallack's, New York, on October 3, 1876.

Marriage (also called *A Bridal Tour*). Unpublished. Produced at Wallack's, New York, on October 1, 1877.

Norah's Vows. Unpublished. Produced at the Theatre Royal, Brighton, on July 6, 1878.

Clarissa Harlowe; or, The History of a Young Lady. Unpublished. Produced at Wallack's, New York, on September 10, 1878. A dramatization of Samuel Richardson's novel.

Spell-Bound. Unpublished. Produced at Wallack's, New York, on February 24, 1879.

Rescued; or, A Girl's Romance. Unpublished. A copyright performance at the King's Cross Theatre, London, on August 27, 1879; produced at Booth's, New York, on September 4, 1879.

Contempt of Court. Unpublished. Produced at Wallack's, New York, on October 4, 1879.

The Amadan. Unpublished. Produced at the Theatre Royal, Richmond, on January 29, 1883.

Vice Versa. Unpublished. Produced at Wallack's Theatre, Springfield, Massachussetts, during May, 1883. Based on *Le Truc d'Arthur* by Duru and Chivot.

Robert Emmet, in *Forbidden Fruit and Other Plays.* A copyright performance at the Prince of Wales's Theatre, Greenwich, England, on November 4, 1884; produced at McVicker's Theatre, Chicago, on November 5, 1884. A revision of an uncompleted script by Frank Marshall.

The Jilt. London and New York: French's Acting Editions, [1904]. Copyright performance at The Elephant and Castle, London, on May 13, 1885; produced at the California Theatre, San Francisco, on May 18, 1885.

The Spae Wife (later called *Cuishla Ma Chree*). Unpublished. Copyright performance at The Elephant and Castle, London, on March 30, 1886; produced at the Hollis Street Theatre, Boston, on February 20, 1888. An adaptation of Scott's novel *Guy Mannering*.

Phyrne; or, The Romance of a Young Wife. Unpublished. Produced at the Baldwin Theatre, San Francisco, on September 12, 1887.

Captain Swift. Unpublished. Produced at the Madison Square Theatre, New York, on December 4, 1888. A revision of the play by Haddon Chambers.

Jimmy Watt (known in New York as *The Tale of a Coat*). Unpublished. Copyright performance at the Elephant and Castle, London, on August 1, 1890; produced at Daly's, New York, on August 14, 1890.

Lend Me Your Wife. Unpublished. Produced at the Boston Museum, Boston, on August 25, 1890. An adaptation of Maurice Desvallières' comedy *Prête-moi ta femme!*

The Chaplain of the Fleet. A printed but not published prompt copy is in the National Library of Ireland. A play of this title was licensed by Lord Chamberlain on December 31, 1890.

99. Unpublished. Produced at the Standard, London, on October 5, 1891.

Jack Weatherby. A printed but not published prompt copy signed by Boucicault is in the National Library of Ireland. I can find no record of its production.

II. Books

The Adventures and Works of Hugh Darley. A three-volume novel which was apparently never published, although it is mentioned as being in the press in Andrews' 1842 edition of *The Irish Heiress*.

The Art of Acting. Introduction by Otis Skinner and Notes by Brander Matthews. New York: Publications of the Dramatic Museum of Columbia University, 1926.

The Art of Acting: A Discussion by Constant Coquelin, Henry Irving, and Dion Boucicault. New York: Publications of the Dramatic Museum of Columbia University, 1926.

Foul Play. With Charles Reade. London: Bradbury, Evans, 1868. Some later editions list Reade alone as author.

The Story of Ireland. Boston: James R. Osgood & Co., 1881. A straightforward, rather dramatically told, short account of twenty-four pages, described by Boucicault as "no more than a brief, perspicuous exhibit of leading events, compiled textually from the best authorities. . . ."

III. Magazine Articles

"The Art of Dramatic Composition," *North American Review*, CXXVI (Jan.–Feb., 1878), 40–52. Boucicault's fullest statement on the subject. His position might be described as a loose Aristotelianism. On many points he is quite traditional, but he also feels that "The liberty of imagination should not be sacrificed to arbitrary restrictions and traditions that lead to dullness and formality. Art is not a church; it is the philosophy of pleasure."

"At the Goethe Society," *North American Review*, CXLVIII (March, 1889), 335–43.

"Coquelin and Hading," *North American Review*, CXLVII (Nov., 1888), 581–83.

"Coquelin-Irving," *North American Review*, CXLV (August, 1887), 158–61.

"The Debut of a Dramatist," *North American Review*, CXLVIII (April, 1889), 454–63. Important autobiographical article.

"The Decline and Fall of the Press," *North American Review*, CXLV (July, 1887), 32–39.

"The Decline of the Drama," *North American Review*, CXXV (Sept., 1877), 235–45. Important commentary on the state of the nineteenth-century theater.

"Early Days of a Dramatist," *North American Review*, CXLVIII (May, 1889), 584–93. Important autobiographical article.

"The Future American Drama," *Arena*, II (Nov., 1890), 641–52. Boucicault's last article, posthumously published.

"Golden Words," *The Era Almanack*. London, 1876.

"Leaves from a Dramatist's Diary," *North American Review*, CXLIX (August, 1889), 228–36. Important autobiographical article.

"Macready in Mobile," *The Era Almanack*. London, 1868.

"Mutilations of Shakespeare, The Poet Interviewed," *North American Review*, CXLVIII (Feb., 1889), 266–68.

"My Pupils," *North American Review*, CXLVII (October, 1888), 435–40. Remarks on acting and on his manner of teaching acting.

"Opera," *North American Review*, CXLIV (April, 1887), 340–48.

"Parnell and the *Times*," *North American Review*, CXLIV (June, 1887), 648–49.

"Rejected Plots," *The Era Almanack*. London, 1883.

"Shakespeare's Influence on the Drama," *North American Review*, CXLVII (Dec., 1888), 681–85.

"Theatres, Halls, and Audiences," *North American Review*, CXLIX (Oct., 1889), 429–36.

SECONDARY SOURCES

ARCHER, WILLIAM. *About the Theatre: Essays and Studies*. London: T. Fisher Unwin, 1886. On Boucicault's opposition to government censorship of drama.

——. *English Dramatists of To-day*. London: Sampson Low & Co., 1882. See pp. 41–46.

AYRES, ALFRED. *Acting and Actors. . . . A Book About Theatre Folk and Theatre Art*. New York: Appleton, 1894. On the Palmer-Boucicault school of acting.

BANCROFT, SQUIRE and MARIE. *The Bancrofts: The Recollections of Sixty Years*. London: John Murray, 1909. Contains some interesting Boucicault letters.

BARNES, J. H. *Forty Years on the Stage: Others (Principally) and Myself*. London: Chapman and Hall, 1914. Information on Boucicault in New York, ca. 1875. See pp. 46–48.

BARTLEY, J. O. *Teague, Shenkin and Sawney*. Cork: Cork University Press, 1954. Good discussion of the Stage Irishman.

BROWN, T. ALLSTON. *A History of the New York Stage*. 3 Vols. New York: Benjamin Blom, Inc., 1964. Superseded by Odell's work, but still useful.

CHESTERTON, G. K. *Avowals and Denials*. London: Methuen & Co., 1934. Short essay on Boucicault as a dramatist.

COLEMAN, JOHN. *Charles Reade, As I Knew Him*. London: Treherne & Co., 1903. Several portraits of Boucicault as an engaging companion, with an irrepressible brogue which he occasionally tried to squelch.

DALTON, FRANK. "Small-Change and Boucicault," *The Dublin Magazine*, I (November 1923), 280–285. Interesting account of Boucicault's appearance and ability as a stage-manager. Also some information concerning his early schooling in Dublin.

DALY, JOSEPH FRANCIS. *The Life of Augustin Daly*. New York: The Macmillan Co., 1917. An account of an attempted collaboration between Boucicault and Bret Harte. Contains several Boucicault letters and working notes on the collaboration. Important for the insight it gives into Boucicault's business-like approach to writing.

DICKENS, CHARLES. *Life of Charles James Mathews*. 2 Vols. London: Macmillan, 1879. Useful background.

DUGGAN, G. C. *The Stage Irishman*. Dublin: Talbot Press, 1937.

FRANCIS, BASIL. *Fanny Kelly of Drury Lane*. London: Rockliff, 1950. Contains the otherwise unnoticed biographical fact that "Lee Morton [*sic*]" was her pupil and protégé, and played the part of Nicholas O'Nib, an Irish schoolmaster, in the curtain raiser *Sum-*

mer and Winter by Morris Barnett, which opened her theater in Dean Street, Soho, on May 25, 1840.

FROHMAN, DANIEL. *Daniel Frohman Presents: An Autobiography.* New York: C. Kendall & W. Sharp, 1935.

————. *Encore.* New York: L. Furman, Inc., 1937. See section entitled "Dion Boucicault," pp. 97–105.

————. *Memories of a Manager.* Garden City, New York: Doubleday, Page & Co., 1911. See particularly pp. 87–90, for remarks on Boucicault.

HARDWICK, J. M. D. *Emigrant in Motley.* London: Rockliff, 1954. On Boucicault's interest in Mrs. Anne Jordan.

JEFFERSON, JOSEPH. *The Autobiography of Joseph Jefferson.* New York: The Century Co., 1890. In particular credits Boucicault for valuable advice on acting; see p. 210.

JOHNSON, ALBERT E. "The Birth of Dion Boucicault," *Modern Drama,* XI (September 1968), 157–163. Contains provocative, if inconclusive, new evidence relating to Boucicault's birthdate and parentage.

KEESE, W. L. *The Life of W. E. Burton.* New York: The Dunlop Society, 1891. On Agnes Robertson.

KENNEY, CHARLES LAMB. *The Career of Dion Boucicault.* New York: The Graphic Co., n.d. This volume, nominally by Boucicault's life-long friend has been attributed to Boucicault himself by his third wife Louise Thorndyke.

KRAUSE, DAVID. "The Theatre of Dion Boucicault, A Short View of His Life and Art," in *The Dolmen Press Boucicault.* Dublin: The Dolmen Press, 1964.

MACLYSAGHT, W. *Death Sails the Shannon: The Authentic Story of The Colleen Bawn.* Tralee: The Kerryman, Ltd., 1953.

MACQUEEN-POPE, W. *Gaiety: Theatre of Enchantment.* London: Greenberg in association with W. H. Allen, n.d.

MACREADY, WILLIAM. *The Diaries of William Charles Macready, 1833–1851.* 2 Vols. London: Chapman & Hall, 1912. Interesting account of a misunderstanding in 1841 with "Lee Moreton," the young author of *London Assurance.* Also valuable for an insight into the character of Macready's friend Dionysius Lardner and for a description of Mrs. Heaviside.

MODJESKA, HELENA. *Memories and Impressions of Helena Modjeska: An Autobiography.* New York: Macmillan, 1910. A valuable short account of Boucicault's "infinite pains" as a stage director; see pp. 349–52. Also an excellent photograph of Dion as "Conn."

MOSES, MONTROSE J. *Famous Actor-Families in America.* New York: T. Y. Crowell & Co., 1906. Chapter on the Boucicaults, bibliography, photos of Dion, Agnes, Aubrey, Nina, and Dot.

Nicoll, Allardyce. *A History of English Drama, 1660–1900:* Vol. IV, *Early Nineteenth Century Drama, 1800–1850.* Cambridge: Cambridge University Press, 1955. See pp. 188–90 for a discussion of Boucicault's early work. See pp. 269–70 for a list of Boucicault's early plays.

————. *A History of English Drama, 1660–1900:* Vol. V, *Late Nineteenth Century Drama, 1850–1900.* Cambridge: Cambridge University Press, 1959. See pp. 84–94 for an appreciative discussion which concludes, "Boucicault's knowledge of the stage and its possibilities was completer than that possessed by any of his contemporaries. . . ." See pp. 267–69 and 779 for a list of Boucicault's later plays.

Odell, George C. D. *Annals of the New York Stage.* 15 Vols. New York: Columbia University Press, 1927. Indispensable.

Ó h Aodha, Micheál. "The Quest for Boucicault" and "The Colleen Bawn and the Dictionary" in *Plays and Places.* Dublin: Progress House, 1961.

Pascoe, Charles Eyre. *The Dramatic List: A Record of the Principal Performances of Living Actors and Actresses of the British Stage.* London: Hardwicke & Bogue, 1879. Contains extracts from newspaper notices of several plays; see pp. 39–49.

Pearce, Charles E. *Madame Vestris and Her Time.* London: Stanley Paul & Co., n.d. See pp. 263–65 for a discussion of the first production of *London Assurance.*

Pemberton, T. Edgar. *Charles Dickens and the Stage: A Record of His Connection with the Drama as Playwright, Actor, and Critic.* London: George Redway, 1888.

————. *The Life of Bret Harte.* London: C. Arthur Pearson, Ltd., 1903.

Quinn, Arthur Hobson. *A History of the American Drama, From the Beginning to the Civil War.* London & New York: Harper & Bros., 1923. See pp. 368–88.

Reade, Charles. *Readiana: Comments on Current Events.* London: Chatto & Windus, 1883. Contains a discussion about the plagiarism in *Foul Play.*

Rowell, George. *The Victorian Theatre, A Survey.* London: Oxford University Press, 1956. See especially pp. 54–57, for discussion of Boucicault.

Ryan, Kate. *Old Boston Museum Days.* Boston: Little, Brown & Co., 1915. See pp. 184–87, for discussion of Boucicault.

Scott, Clement. *The Drama of Yesterday & To-day.* 2 Vols. London: Macmillan, 1899. Quotes Boucicault's preface to *London Assurance* and gives an account of the origin of the play; see Vol. 1, pp. 92–109.

SOTHERN, EDWARD H. *The Melancholy Tale of "Me," My Remembrances.* New York: Charles Scribner's Sons, 1916.

STODDART, J. H. *Recollections of a Player.* New York: The Century Co., 1902.

THOMPSON, VANCE. "Dion Boucicault" in *Famous American Actors of To-day.* Ed. F. E. McKay & C. E. L. Wingate. New York: Thomas Y. Crowell Co., 1896. See Vol. 1, pp 80–87.

VANBRUGH, IRENE. *To Tell My Story.* London: Hutchinson & Co., n.d. Miss Vanbrugh was the wife of Boucicault's son, Dot. She includes on pp. 39–40 Boucicault's important letter to his mother after the success of *London Assurance.* Her account of Boucicault's "The Wearing of the Green" is plagiarized from Townsend Walsh.

WALLACK, LESTER. *Memories of Fifty Years.* New York: Scribner's, 1889. Boucicault mentioned *passim.*

WALSH, TOWNSEND. *The Career of Dion Boucicault.* New York: The Dunlop Society, 1915. The first major work on Boucicault. Although erroneous in many instances, all later critics must be indebted to it.

WILDE, OSCAR. *The Letters of Oscar Wilde.* Ed. Rupert Hart-Davis. New York: Harcourt, Brace & World, Inc., 1962. Contains on pp. 92–93 an interesting letter from Boucicault on Wilde. See also Wilde's letter to Clara Morris on pp. 70–71.

WINTER, WILLIAM. *The Life of David Belasco.* 2 Vols. New York: Moffat, Yard & Co., 1918. Boucicault mentioned *passim.*

———. *Vagrant Memories: Being Further Recollections of Other Days.* New York: George H. Doran & Co., 1915.

———. *Other Days.* New York: Moffat, Yard & Co., 1908. See pp. 124–51 for a discussion of Boucicault. Winter's caustic view of Boucicault seems considerably tinged by his own spleen and fustiness.

Special mention must be given to the unpublished doctoral dissertation (Pennsylvania, 1951) by Julius H. Tolson, "Dion Boucicault." Although I disagree with many of its conclusions, it is the fullest study of the plays; and I have been much indebted to it in these pages.

Index